7 Attitudes of the Helping Heart

How to Live Out Your Faith and Care for the Poor

John Christopher Frame

7 Attitudes of the Helping Heart: How to Live Out Your Faith and Care for the Poor by John Christopher Frame

Copyright © 2021 by John Christopher Frame

Visit the author's website at http://www.johnchristopherframe.com

ISBN: 978-1-954709-00-3

Praise for 7 Attitudes of the Helping Heart

"This book is like a window into people's lives around the world, with sensory details that help us empathize with circumstances that we otherwise struggle to imagine."

—Rev. Matthew Ingalls, Author of *The Upside Down Way: Following Jesus through the Gospel of Luke*

"Frame's personal story, mingled with the stories of friends in Cambodia trapped in crippling poverty, creates a compelling narrative for his solid teaching on how we all can nurture qualities in ourselves in order to better care for others in need with a truly empowered, serving, and loving mindset."

—Jamie Aten, PhD, Founder & Executive Director, Humanitarian Disaster Institute, Wheaton College, and author of *A Walking Disaster: What Surviving Katrina and Cancer Taught Me About Faith and Resilience*

"Personal encounters with the poor are often a struggle for Christians. So much of our faith tells us to help. But how? Such encounters can leave us conflicted and confused. In *7 Attitudes of the Helping Heart,* John Christopher Frame invites us to feel the tensions of such experiences. He then explores how some of the core virtues of our faith—compassion, empathy, and holiness among them—can give us wisdom in how to navigate tricky ethical situations. In the process, Frame provides a glimpse of how God can work through the body of believers in a world full of suffering, and the joy that can result for all involved. It is an inspirational read."

—Stephen Offutt, PhD, Professor of Development Studies, Asbury Theological Seminary

"This book is full of stories of needy persons and generous Christians responding with compassion and love. These stories from around the world both show how we struggle to be generous and also encourage us to move toward greater generosity."

—Ronald Sider, PhD, President emeritus, Evangelicals for Social Action, and author of *Rich Christians in an Age of Hunger*

Acknowledgments

The author thanks the following people who provided input to this book and his other work over the past year: Ayşegül Frame, Bonnie Newell, Chad Allen and members of BookCamp, Christy Distler, Derek Doepker, Don Brewster, Fran Bennett, Gene and Marsha Frame, Jess Templeman, Jim Lyon, Jonathan Smith, Josh Deeter, Kelsey McCoy, Lawana Partlow, Luke de Pulford, Nancy Landes, Pam Suiter, Richard Weston, Steven D. Cohen, and Tim Leary. Finally, the author thanks Sak, Theary, and Pun, whose words in this book help us all understand the world a little better.

Contents

Foreword

By Jim Lyon

I n Luke's Gospel, we read that Jesus visited His home-town, Nazareth. Invited to speak in the synagogue, He was handed a scroll with the words of Isaiah the prophet. In this moment, He defined Himself and His ministry. As the crowd sat in silence, everyone looking at him, Jesus read the theme sentence of His whole message: "The Spirit of the Lord is upon me, for he has anointed me to bring Good News to the poor" (Luke 4:18a NLT).

The poor. This was His audience of choice—the focus of His coming, His teaching, His love. And this simple truth has often made me uneasy and uncomfortable. Troubled, really. It's not because Jesus straight-up declared His heart for the poor, but instead because I don't know how to actually follow Him in this. I want to, I think. But I don't know how.

Or maybe I don't really want to.

There's so much about what Jesus said that I don't actually do, that His words can routinely make me feel uncomfortable. How about that Golden Rule, for instance? "Do to others whatever you would like them to do to you. This is the essence of all that is taught in the law and the prophets" (Matthew 7:12 NLT).

Yes, I'm a nice guy who generally treats others with

kindness, because that is the way I'd like to be treated. And, after all, it just seems like the right thing to do.

But what if I was poor? Like, really poor? What if I had been born into systemic poverty in the developing world, without any hope of moving up or out? What if I wasn't certain how to provide for myself or my family? How would I like others to treat me, with my hand outstretched, my eyes pleading for relief? And what does that say to me when I am the one seeing another's outstretched hand? Ouch. I would prefer not to have to deal with it.

Jesus talks a lot about "the poor." So does the whole of Scripture. People who are poor are front and center, it seems, in the heart and mind of God.

John Christopher Frame talks a lot about "the poor" too. He does so because the Spirit of Jesus has caused him to wrestle with the dilemma of economic and cultural privilege in the face of desperate poverty on multiple continents. This book is his way of working out how to think through some of this. It's for anyone who takes Jesus seriously and sees what He sees, feels what He feels.

Frame knows that even referring to others as "the poor" can imply a certain stereotyping or prejudice. He knows that we are not seen by God as the sum of our circumstances or presentation; he knows that, with or without material means, the *imago Dei* is in every one of us. Still, it is "the poor" to whom Jesus felt most supremely called.

Frame's life has been one of adventure and discovery. Reading this book is to explore your own heart on the stage of vivid descriptions of faraway places and the people he has met there—people whose impoverished journeys will dare and inspire. Reading this book will place you on the streets of Delhi and on obscure corners in Cambodia; it will take you to London rowhouses, and to your own wrestling mat.

You will experience the author's struggle and know that it is yours as well. You will ask yourself questions. And you will want to sit down with others and talk. Reading each chapter, I wanted to call Frame on my mobile and talk—or call anyone and just talk. Reading this book will invite you—maybe compel you—to talk through your challenges, questions, and opportunities with someone else.

In the end, you will want to talk to Jesus. Because, if you want to truly follow Him, you will not be able to do so without speaking to "the poor." At the end of the day—yes, that Last Day at the end of the age—Jesus will remind us all: "Whatever you did for one of the least of these brothers and sisters of mine, you did for me" (Matthew 25:40).

Ouch.

7 Attitudes of the Helping Heart will prepare you for that day. It will help you not just then, but also today—right here, right now—as well. And it might just help you become the answer to someone else's heart-cry, to someone else also loved by Jesus.

Jim Lyon
General Director, Church of God Ministries,
and Host of ViewPoint

Chapter 1

Introduction: Facing Internal Challenges

"Mister, can you buy some food for my baby?" A woman was standing in the street, holding an infant, as I left the budget hotel in Delhi, India, that I'd checked into the night before.

Nearby, stray cows foraged for edible garbage on the road while men hawked cheap toys. The air smelled of charcoal and sometimes like an outhouse. *Tuk-tuks*—small taxis that look something like green-and-yellow golf carts with three wheels—beeped their horns. On this same street the night before, a motorcycle with two young men came bulleting to my toes as if I were the finish line of a race. They laughed. But I was irked, overwhelmed by the chaos and worried about finding my hotel.

I would see this woman and her baby nearly every day of my three-week stay. Sometimes she'd walk in the middle of the street; sometimes she'd stand on the side.

We spoke briefly. I was nice, the way you are when you meet a stranger for the first time and you want to leave a good impression. It gave me time to stall and process what was going on. *Do I want to help this woman? How much am I comfortable giving?*

I followed her to a tiny walk-up shop, and she told the shopkeeper in Hindi what she wanted. The man put a few items on the counter and told me the total price.

Wow, that's a lot of money. How can that be right? It may not have seemed expensive to most tourists, but I lived on the cheap. I was in India for a school-related project, and I hadn't had a full-time job in six years.

I picked up each item for a closer look. It wasn't that I didn't care about the woman and her needs; it was that I felt trapped. On one hand, I wanted to help the woman. I wanted to live out my faith. But on the other hand, I wondered if I was being cheated. I should've been the one choosing how to spend my money, not a stranger. I felt awkward and no longer in control.

Right or wrong, I told them which of the products I was willing to buy. When I walked away, I was happier about leaving the woman than about any good I may have done.

A few days later, the woman saw me on the street again. This time she asked me to buy her a blanket. Though I didn't want to face her again, I felt I should be nice and help her.

She is in need. It's January and it's cold. She and her family lived in a tent, she'd told me.

I followed her again, this time to another shop, where we looked at blankets. "How about this one?" I asked.

She held up a more expensive one and started talking about it, how nice it was. Mine wasn't good enough. Nevertheless, I tried to convince her otherwise, as if I was the seller and she was the buyer. "It's beautiful, good," I said.

She persisted.

Why does she want the most expensive one? How much is this going to cost me? Why is she so pushy? My own fight against my lack of generosity, coupled with uncertainty about if or how to help this woman again, was complicated by the kind of feeling you get when you think someone is out to get as much of your money as they can. The truth is, I was thinking more about my money than about the woman and her needs. My aim was to leave the store spending the least amount possible. It seemed she was seeing right through me.

Then something happened.

"Greedy," one of the workers in the shop said, pointing to the woman like he knew all her secrets.

It was as if the man was trying to help me, be on my side, involve himself in something he didn't believe was right. To me, the message was clear: he was exposing her as a greedy beggar.

Looking back, I wonder now if she even needed a blanket. I later learned about women in Cambodia who hold babies and ask tourists to buy them baby formula. The women then return it to the store for cash. Perhaps the woman I was trying to help was doing the same thing. Maybe she had shown me the same blanket previous tourists had bought her, in a cycle the worker wanted to stop. Or maybe she *did* need a blanket and she was showing me the one that she knew would be just right. The one that would keep her family warm.

Right or wrong, this time I left the shop without buying anything.

Our Internal Struggles

Many of us wonder how to help people in poverty, or if we even can. We wonder if they deserve our help. *Maybe they're an addict. Maybe they're trying to scam me.* If we agree to help someone, we ask ourselves if we made the right decision. If we decline, we regret we didn't help. We question whether people are *really* poor. We debate with ourselves whether the small bit we could do would make any difference. We may even battle against the beast of resistance within us: our own self-centeredness, lack of generosity, and apathy—the little voice that says, *My money is mine.* It tells us we don't need to share what we have, that we don't need to help people we don't know. We feel bad about this.

Some of us overthink how to help people living in poverty. Some of us don't think about it enough.

Yet there's no question that many people are poor. While you may not consider yourself rich, if you're reading this book, you're probably better off than the 2 billion people who drink water from a source contaminated with feces.[1] And the 700 million who live on less than $1.90 a day.[2]

No one chooses to be poor. Most are born into it. Its causes are complex. We hear statistics, like those above, but they seem so unreal and far away. We think we could never do anything to really help. Plus, we have our own families to look after, our own rent or mortgage to pay. We have enough problems of our own, we think.

The truth is that, for many of us, helping people who are poor is a side thought, something we don't think about enough. But in the world is great need that deserves our attention. Plus, as Christians, we feel we should care about people. We feel guilty about not helping the poor. We know the Bible calls us to love others. We know when we help people in need, we serve God better.

Still, with little or no contact with those who are poor, it's hard for many of us to conceptualize what poverty is, the daily challenges of those who live it, and how best to respond. So where do we begin? How do we begin?

This book brings the experiences of people in poverty to life and provides a framework for how you can begin your own journey of helping those who are poor. We're going to explore seven Attitudes of the Helping Heart that, when developed in your life, will help you live out your faith so you can better support those in need.

---

1 "Drinking-water," *World Health Organization*, https://www.who.int/news-room/fact-sheets/detail/drinking-water.

2 "Poverty Overview," *The World Bank*, https://www.worldbank.org/en/topic/poverty/overview.

Nurturing these attitudes will empower you to battle the beast of resistance that leads you away from those you feel, down deep, you should care about. This book will assist you in developing a way of caring that helps you powerfully impact those in need. That's because caring more for the poor makes it easier to help them.

Finally, accompanying us along our reading journey are three people I met in Cambodia who share their own stories, helping us understand poverty from a first-person perspective: a Buddhist monk-turned-security-guard with a singing voice that could have made him famous; a church volunteer who works seventy hours a week in a garment factory making the clothes you and I wear; and an eighty-one-year-old great-grandmother who sold groceries outside her front door and helped organize building the only church in her village. They share their lives with us, in their own words, offering an unforgettable peek into the world of people living in poverty. Their stories are woven throughout this book, helping us better dive into the seven Attitudes of the Helping Heart, so we can better live out our faith and care for the poor.

Let's meet them now.

Taking It to the Next Level

This book's companion study guide is available as a free gift to you. It can be downloaded via the link below and will help you better integrate into your life the ideas in this book. Furthermore, another excellent way to get more out of this book is to tell your friends you're reading it, and discuss your thoughts about it together.

Inside the companion study guide, you will get:

✓ Reflective questions

✓ Prayers

✓ Bible passages

✓ Challenges to complete

✓ Areas to journal

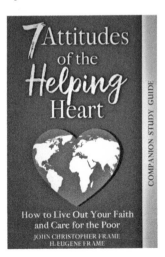

Download the free study guide at:
http://www.johnchristopherframe.org

Chapter 2

Meeting the Poor: Seeing Similarities Among Our Differences

Introducing Sak, the Security Guard

S ak Dong was the security guard at the apartment in Cambodia where my wife and I lived while I completed research for my PhD. He'd sit outside all day in a straight wood chair that matched a long wood table where he kept his walkie talkie, billy club, and a small stack of notebooks with colorful covers. There was also a security log where he'd jot down what happened each day.

13:00 – Delivery man dropped something off
13:30 – Helped wash Dan's car

Once or twice his pen ran out of ink and I bought him a new one. Office supplies didn't seem to come with the job.

Sak was about thirty years old. He had an innocent-looking face, and eyes that told the story of a gentle person who wanted to get ahead but couldn't because of his own life circumstances. "I don't blame anyone for my poverty. I only blame myself," he told me. He lamented about not having a better education or a specific set of skills. "If I had a better education, then I would not be poor like this."

Sak maintained a cheerful smile, and there wasn't a day he didn't show up for work. I'd sometimes sit next to him at his table—he in his uniform with a tie and a decorative white rope around his left shoulder, and me in my t-shirt, shorts, and sandals.

We'd talk about the day, which mostly related to what we ate. Sak cooked rice in a rice cooker near his work table, and he'd buy something for fifty cents at the farmers' market to go with it, like stewed vegetables and pork skins with hair bristles. He'd carry it from the market in a clear plastic bag, like a goldfish in water, and he'd stretch it out to last all day.

Each day, he'd show me the book he was studying to learn English, and he'd ask me questions about the new words he was learning. Sak's English was very limited, and I only knew a few words of the Cambodian language, enough to say hello and buy things like mangos and bananas at the farmers' market. He thought my wife's name was "My Wife." So he'd say things like, "How's my wife?" He never pronounced the last letter of a word, though, so he'd actually say, "How's my why?"

Sak and his small family lived in one room with another relative. Everyone who lived in the building shared a common toilet. Despite the struggles he'd faced—including losing his father in war—he remained hopeful that someday, maybe, he'd have a better life. Even more, he hoped for a better life for his son.

In the Words of Sak, the Security Guard

Reflections on work

*E*ven though my job is not hard labor, it's long hours. I work twelve hours a day. Once, I worked thirty-six hours straight. I worked my normal twelve-hour shift, then I covered the next shift for the other security guard who couldn't make it to work. Then in the morning, it was my shift again. So I had to work another twelve hours. The base salary each month is $100, working twelve hours per day, six days a week. I get more if I work overtime and earn a bonus.

Working as a security guard—we don't have any specific skills. If we stop working as a security guard, then it's hard for us to find another kind of job. But if I worked in construction, then I'd learn skills, and there'd be a chance to become a manager.

I feel that now I'm making just enough to get by. I don't have money for saving for the future. So I want to have a better job. And if I can, I want to have my own small business, or get a motorcycle and carriage—a tuk-tuk—so I can run my own taxi business. That type of work would give me freedom as well.

Introducing Theary,
the Garment Factory Worker

Theary worked at a garment factory that made shirts for people in other countries, like the United States. Her job was inspecting the clothes—quality control—and, in some ways, her job was easy, she said. In other ways, it was difficult, as she worked seven days a week with mandatory overtime. Like Sak, the security guard, she'd had challenges in life from an early age, including the death of her mother when she was a child. And then her father was put into prison.

Theary was a friend of a translator who assisted me in Cambodia. When I met her, in 2013, she was thirty years old and had never used a computer. Though many others in Cambodia used social media, she didn't know how to use the internet and didn't have a Facebook account.

Theary was tall and thin, with long black hair. She spoke confidently and didn't pretend to be overly happy. Like most Cambodians, she ate rice three times a day. And if working long hours at the factory wasn't enough, she made soy milk in the evenings and sold it on the side. Despite the difficulties she faced, she had a hopeful future. "I'm saving money for tailoring school," she told me. "My plan is to stop working in the factory."

Yet, even though she had a loving fiancé, was setting money aside for her education, and had what seemed to be a thought-out plan for a better future, she was afraid that her dream wouldn't come true. Despite her preparation and excitement, she worried, "I'm afraid whether or not I'll have a chance to become a tailor and have my own business."

In the Words of Theary, the Garment Factory Worker

Reflections on childhood difficulties

*M*y mom passed away when I was seven years old. She had a heart attack. I still remember that time. When my mother was alive, I never felt we had life difficulties; but when she passed away, some hardships came. When I got sick, no one was there to look after me. And if I wanted to buy something, sometimes I would ask my brothers, but they didn't give me what I asked for. I cried a lot. I didn't feel loved. My dad worked far away. He'd come to visit us only about once a month. So one of my brothers was sort of like my parent. I'd ask him to buy some books, but he didn't give me money. "This is all that we've got," he'd say.

When I was young, I liked to pretend I was cooking. My friends and I would cut leaves for making pretend food. And I would also cut pretend clothes from the leaves of a tree for dolls I'd make. I'd take some moist dirt and shape it into something that looked like a little person. Then I'd put it under the sun. Then I'd cut several leaves with a knife and put them together on the doll, using a thin piece of bamboo like a string to dress the doll. When I played like that, my dad saw me and he bought some toys for me—like a doll that had clothes and shoes.

Introducing Pun, the Great-Grandmother

Pun was a great-grandmother who lived on a dirt road in the woods, miles from the closest town. In her village were a school as well as a church with a metal roof and outside walls with faded yellow paint. Mildew stains across the bottom told the story of the church being flooded during the rainy season.

When we talked the first time, Pun and I sat outside on red plastic chairs in front of the church. Sometimes people would interrupt us to talk to her. As we spoke, children in school uniforms played nearby. They chased each other and laughed.

Pun was feisty, with short gray hair, and her lips would press over her gums when she laughed, showing her wide, toothless smile. She used her hands when she talked, sometimes repeating something again and again, like how she wanted a new school for the village.

Pun and her son sold candy, cold soda, groceries, and household items just outside the doors of their homes—a common practice in Cambodia to earn income. It was also important because, as far as I could see, there was no other shop around to purchase anything.

Pun was an entrepreneur, buying things, like a motorbike, at a low price and selling them for a profit. I had met her through the founder of a Christian faith-based organization that had provided some microloans to help her in her business ventures.

"I know everyone who lives around here because I've been living here since I was born," she told me. "For me, the best part of living in this village is that I get to live near the church. I don't have to walk far." Despite enduring the normal aches and pains that came with her age, Pun had an attitude of perseverance and grit—necessary in order to survive and prosper in a small village plunged into war years before.

In the Words of Pun, the Great-Grandmother

Reflections on early life

I don't really remember the exact year I was born, but I know I'm around eighty-one years old. I was born in the village I still live in. My house back then was tiny. It was a really tiny old wooden house. It wasn't even like a house.

My mom had fifteen children and only four of us are left—I am the oldest. When I was a child, I didn't have any toys to play with, or anything. I just worked with my dad at the farm because I was the oldest.

Nowadays, in my free time, I take care of the animals and farm, but I don't really have free time. Since I was young, until now, I've always worked.

I was twenty years old when I got married. My husband was from the village next to mine. We knew each other and fell in love. Then our parents arranged the marriage for us. My husband was a hard-working young man and didn't drink alcohol. We really loved each other. He passed away when he was sixty-three.

Life is happy, but there is sadness sometimes.

Understanding Our Similarities

Pun was right. Life is happy, but there is also sadness in the world.

A few years before my wife and I lived in Cambodia, I completed a short Bible history course one summer at a college in Jerusalem. Afterward, I followed in the footsteps of a classmate who, before our course had begun, had solo-ventured through Egypt. Despite the diarrhea-related emergencies he suffered during his trip, it sounded like an adventure I'd like to have too.

I crossed the Israeli border on foot and walked into Egypt, starting my journey. I snorkeled in the Red Sea, joined a group in the middle of the night to hike Mount Sinai to reach the summit before sunrise, traded my Dollar Tree sunglasses for a knickknack a teenager was trying to sell me next to the Sphinx, and boarded an all-night train to see the Valley of the Kings and Queens.

One of the briefest moments I had in Egypt has always stayed with me. After checking into a hostel in Cairo, following a long bus ride through the Sinai Peninsula, I found a McDonald's and then wandered the streets, my mouth probably gaping with awe at the masses of people everywhere. The sun had set and the day had cooled. It was the time everyone came out and did their shopping. Pedestrians filled the sidewalks. Cars clogged the streets. A small girl approached me, tapped me on the arm, and pointed to the

McDonald's cup of apple juice I was holding. She held out her hand, reaching for it, and I gave it to her. Then she ran off.

I think of that experience as one of my first face-to-face encounters with someone who was *really* poor. It has stuck in my mind because of the desperation I sensed behind her desire for a leftover drink from a stranger. Or maybe she didn't ask me for a drink because she was thirsty, but rather because she didn't get many opportunities to have something from McDonald's—luxury food in some countries. Maybe she thought I was drinking Coca-Cola. At least it was a distraction from the regular burden of begging that I imagined she was accustomed to. Really, though, I'll never know her needs.

Later in that trip, I rented a bicycle for the day, not realizing how far it was to where I wanted to go or just how hot it was going to be that day. While crossing the Nile River on a ferry with the bike next to me, I met a man who operated a taxi service with his personal car. I accepted his offer to drive me around, the bicycle strapped on top.

At some point, his employee began driving, and this man invited me to have tea with his family. When I agreed, we went to his home—a hut of sorts, with mud walls and a dirt floor. He smiled and kindly invited me inside to meet his family. I sat in their living room, on something like a wooden bed with rough posts and a thin mat, next to a TV with a cable box on top. A large poster of a white baby was tacked to the wall, along with something like a carpet. His young daughters wore long red dresses, and their heads were covered with black hijabs. His wife served me tea in a small glass, along with a cookie. I had never been in a house made of dirt, and I looked carefully at the outside wall, touching it, before leaving.

Despite our many differences, I think that taxi driver and I shared several things in common. An interest in sharing time with others. The giving and receiving of hospitality. A desire to know and be known. Love for our families. Hope for health, happiness, and prosperity. An interest in serving God.

These were all similar, if not the same.

I was never quite sure why the taxi driver invited me to have tea at his home, though I know hospitality in many parts of the world can be different than where I grew up. Spontaneous invitations, drinking tea, and passing time together—even with strangers—seems normal in Egypt.

Understanding similarities we have with people who seem very different from us isn't always easy. Maybe it's because we often focus on what we see on the outside rather than what's on the inside. We look at what people have, or don't have, rather than *who* they are—their wants, hopes, disappointments, memories, and feelings. We don't see the invisible aspects of their lives—their relationships, the love they have for a child, the joy they get from friends, their physical pains, their sadness from loss, their hunger for food.

What's on the outside may look very different, but what's on the inside is nearly the same for all of us. Remembering our commonalities can help us see beyond our differences.

When we think of people living in poverty, it's helpful to remember that their lives and characteristics should be distinguished from their economic poverty. For this reason, I typically refer in this book to "people living in poverty," or a similar phrase, as this emphasizes *people*, rather than something that characterizes them, like their economic status. Poverty is not the characteristic by which people should be solely identified, their main identity. There is much more about them. Poverty is something they're going through, or, for many, something they endure their whole lives. It's not who they are.[3]

As a leader of a nonprofit organization recently told me, people who are poor are often seen as part of one large category, while those of us who are not poor are known for our individuality. But the truth is we are each unique individuals who have emotions, fears, love, and experiences that make us who we are.

Seeing People as God Views Them

As human beings, it is not natural for us to deeply care about strangers, or really to even think much about them. Yet, all of us are made in the image of God. He knows the number of hairs on the heads of strangers just like he knows the number of mine and yours. God loves them, cares about them, and suffers with them. One of life's biggest challenges, I think, is seeing people as God views them, especially the billions in

---

3 I thank Fran Bennett, my doctoral supervisor at the University of Oxford, who explored this topic with me while I was writing this book, and inspired the ideas in this paragraph.

the world we'll never meet personally. God loves everyone, whether we know them or not, including those who are poor and in need.

The remainder of this book explores seven Attitudes of the Helping Heart—Gratitude, Humility, Empathy, Compassion, Generosity, Holiness, and Hope—that, when developed, can help us live out our faith so we can better help those in need. Nurturing these attitudes in our lives helps us remember how God loves and suffers with those who are poor, whomever or wherever they are. They help us see people as God sees them.

Taking It to the Next Level

Review the reflective questions, recite the prayer, read the Bible passage, take the challenge, and write your personal reflections in the free *7 Attitudes of the Helping Heart Companion Study Guide.*

Download the free study guide at:
http://www.johnchristopherframe.org

In the Words of Sak, the Security Guard

Reflections on growing up in Cambodia

*W*hen I was a child, I didn't have a bicycle. My best friend lived about a minute's walk from me. We didn't have money, so we would make a toy car out of mud or wood. If it was mud, we'd dry it after we made it and then we'd cut a flip-flop in a circle to make wheels. We'd attach a string to it and pull it. It lasted longer if we didn't let it get wet or put anything heavy on top of it.

I have one brother and one sister. When I was a child, we would catch fish and crabs in the rice fields. We also had a pond behind the house. In the dry season, our family sold water from it. The water was quite clean. We'd put the water on a cart pulled by a horse. Some families were serious about hygiene, so they boiled the water first, like my family. Other families would just drink it with ice to make it cold.

During that time, the serious illness was measles. It seemed most of the children in our area, when they got it, died. It's like my life is very valuable or lucky, or something, because I also had measles, but I didn't die.

My first life dream was to be in a circus. When I was a child, I liked to bend my body and pretend I was in a circus with friends. My second dream was that I would be a singer. Sometimes I feel regret because I wanted to become a singer but it couldn't happen. My friends used to encourage

*me. "Why don't you apply on a TV station to be a singer?"
they'd say. I just thought,* No, not yet. *I was busy with work,
doing this and that. I kept delaying. That's why I feel regret.
I should have tried out, but I wasn't able to do it.*

*Now, I just sing by myself. Sometimes, during parties or
weddings, I get on the stage and sing for everybody. I feel
relief at those times—that I can let other people know about
my voice. I am happy when I have a chance to sing on the
stage—to show my talents to others. I am happy then.*

In the Words of Theary,
the Garment Factory Worker

Reflections on adolescence and current life

I went to school through the ninth grade, and then I stopped. This is my biggest regret. I regret I didn't finish my education. I liked school. The school was about three miles from my house, and I rode my bicycle. Each day, we all had to give a little money to the teachers. I don't know what the money was used for, but we all gave the same amount. Many times, I forgot to take the money, so I'd tell my teacher I'd give double money the next day.

Then my family had a problem, and I stopped going to school. My dad was working for the government. One day, he was with his friend, and they went somewhere. His friend left him and told him to wait. Pretty soon, a police officer came by, and my dad was accused of having drugs on the table. They said he was a drug dealer. So my father was arrested and put in prison—for ten years. When my father was in prison, I visited him, but only twice a year. Since I had no one to support me, I had to start working in the garment factory.

My dad is out of prison now and he stays with me. He has diabetes. We live in a small rental room—just one room. We have a TV, and I like watching TV. Sometimes I watch it alone, or with family or friends. I especially like cooking programs from Cambodia, as well as fashion shows from other countries. I also like watching concerts on TV, listening to Cambodian music from a few years back—music from my childhood, like from 1979–1993. I don't like the current music.

I enjoy doing housework, cleaning the house, mopping the floor, washing dishes. I like all of that. I wash my clothes by hand in a large bucket. I put some water and a little detergent and wash them with my hands. I use a brush for some clothes, and just my hands for things like T-shirts.

In the Words of Pun, the Great-Grandmother

Reflections on family life in Cambodia

I'm very happy living in this village. I'm happy I live next door to the church. Some of my children live nearby, and some are in the next village. Two of them are in Thailand to make a living. One of my children left the kids here and went there to work. The other one took the whole family to Thailand. They sell chickens and work in construction. They often work overtime to save money.

It's hard to make a living here, so that's why my children had to go to Thailand—to make more income and have a better lifestyle.

I have thirty grandchildren and fifteen great-grandchildren. Some want to study and others want to go to Thailand. I want my grandchildren and great-grandchildren to study and then get a really good job—not a low-skilled job in Thailand.

It's better here in Cambodia now than before. People have a better standard of living now, and that makes me happier and happier.

Chapter 3

Gratitude and Humility: Living in the In-Between

When I was a student, I once took a Christian Ethics course that had an assignment requiring an experiential component. Each of us was to participate in some kind of activity that helped us reflect on an ethical issue. The topic I chose was the Christian moral response to hunger, and I decided not to eat for seven days. I called it a hunger simulation. It would be an opportunity to feel hunger, I'd thought, to experience some of the struggles of people in poverty.[4]

I lost twelve pounds. The week felt longer than most. Walking upstairs became more difficult. I was less eager to greet people in the hallway. Each day, I'd think, *Five more days until I can eat again. Four more days. Three more days.*

---

4   I am a healthy person, and though some people choose to fast for long periods of time, I believe fasting for shorter periods than what I did, if you are healthy, provides a better experience.

Despite not eating that week, I realized that other forms of nourishment came from friends. Talking with people "fed" me. Conversations distracted me from my empty stomach. And I knew my experience was temporary. I'd be back to my normal self soon.

That semester, I read passages in the Bible that related to hunger and helping those who are poor, such as 1 John 3:17–18: "If anyone has material possessions and sees a brother or sister in need but has no pity on them, how can the love of God be in that person? Dear children, let us not love with words or speech but with actions and in truth." I read books and articles, and remember a sentence from Ronald J. Sider's *Rich Christians in an Age of Hunger* that stood out to me: "Regardless of what we do or say at 11:00 A.M. Sunday morning, affluent people who neglect the poor are not the people of God."[5]

Another author argued that, through fasting, God wants us to feel hunger and the weariness that comes from not eating. If we don't ever experience it, even briefly, he said, how can we learn to care for those in need? Fasting allows for a short glimpse into the world of the hungry.[6]

---

5 Ronald J. Sider, *Rich Christians in an Age of Hunger: A Biblical Study* (Downers Grove: Intervarsity Press, 1977), 82. A revised and updated version of this book was published in 2015.

6 Mark Buchanan, "Go Fast and Live: Hunger as a Spiritual Discipline," *Christian Century* 118, no. 7 (February 28, 2001): 16-20. p. 19. Quote: "Fasting is meant to scour our gut. It is God's intent that we feel the pangs of hunger, the gnawing emptiness, the dizziness and weariness. That's how a third of the world lives. And if we never live that way, even briefly, how will we learn to care for the least of these? ... Fasting gives us a small taste of what their world is like, a taste we will never get if we do not for a time forsake the taste of food."

Yet, I also learned how proper action to help people in poverty requires more than just a personal response of simple living. Social structures and public policies require change in order to really help solve the world's biggest problems, like hunger. As I reflected on the topic, I thought about how we forget that most of the world's poor have no way out of their current situation. Because of their life circumstances, they can't get ahead. Some can't even make ends meet.

I thought about how we who live in rich countries think nothing of spending large amounts on food for ourselves. However, we may hesitate when it comes to providing for people living in poverty. We spend money on elegant foods, when many around the world do not have the basics. These things bothered me.

I also thought about how, in our abundance, we often overeat, which in some small way seems to indicate there is plenty for everyone. I thought about how overeating could actually be a form of wasting food. I thought about how when we overeat, we consume what others don't have and what we don't need. Also, when we overeat, we may forget about those who don't have food to waste.

I also reflected on the topic theologically. I thought about how choosing not to waste food might be a spiritual act where we acknowledge there is a hunger problem, and we remember those living in poverty. This could also help us reflect on our abundance. Finally, I recalled how, along with physical nourishment needed to sustain our bodies, Jesus, as "the bread that came down from heaven" (John 6:58 NLT), is our spiritual nourishment. Jesus is the giver of hope that days will come when hunger is gone forever and a heavenly feast will never end.

I reflected on how we, in Western society, live in a bubble, isolated from problems that affect much of the world's population. For example, according to the most recent statistics, 821 million people, or one out of nine people in the world, don't have sufficient food.[7] I feared that we in the church were not fully touched by the severity of these problems. Instead, we're engrossed in our own lives, victims of our own ways of living.

The In-Between

If I were to reflect on the topic of hunger all over again, I would probably think more about gratitude for food, and all the things I've been given in life. It is because of this that I have access to all the food I would ever need or want. The truth is, I have everything I need. Because of this, I feel grateful yet am aware I have opportunities, possessions, and access to services that many others don't have. In short, these are privileges.

As people who live in the West, we enjoy many privileges. We drink clean water from the tap. We have freedom. Our human rights are protected. We know English as our native language. We have easy access to the internet. If you're like

---

7 "Food," *United Nations*, https://www.un.org/en/sections/issues-depth/food/index.html; and "Global hunger continues to rise, new UN report says," *World Health Organization*, https://www.who.int/news-room/detail/11-09-2018-global-hunger-continues-to-rise---new-un-report-says.

me, you're privileged in other ways too. You've received an education. You have loved ones or friends who provide you emotional support. You don't feel socially excluded because of poverty. Your growth hasn't been stunted from childhood malnourishment.

We have little control over what we've been given in life, such as our nationality. What we have that others don't have can even position us for more opportunities. For example, growing up in a loving family often helps a child become a healthy, educated person who can acquire a decent job. No doubt, some of us have more privileges than others. All of us benefit from the opportunities we've been given, whether we understand them as privileges or not. We may overlook their significance or even take them for granted.

For me, I think it's important to balance my own privileges with a recognition of what they are—gifts that many others don't have and never will, such as my education, family, job, freedom, healthcare, and cash in my pocket. I'm thankful for all I have. Yet I have opportunities and possessions others don't. Therefore, I'm privileged. As such, I feel a level of responsibility, knowing that many don't have what I have. In fact, so many have so little. So I live in a tension, being thankful on the one hand and feeling uncomfortable on the other. I live in the in-between.

Living in the in-between means we understand our privileges with a heart that is both gracious and humble. We're always thankful, even amid our own difficulties. Having a spirit of both gratitude and humility can help us be a little more in touch with the everyday problems of others. It can help us remember those in need.

Furthermore, being humble helps us remember that, even though we're privileged, we're also vulnerable to losing what we have. Our lives can drastically change. Companies downsize and employees lose their jobs. Accidents happen and people become disabled. Infectious diseases can cause fear and death. Fires and natural disasters destroy homes. The things we are grateful for can be lost. The protections, comforts, and securities we have today may not be ours tomorrow. That should keep us humble.

Humility helps us understand that we may not be that far from the same kinds of difficulties affecting others. Humility helps us recognize our own fragility, how easy it is to lose some or all of what we have. We might be close to poverty ourselves.

Just as we who live comfortably now are susceptible to hardships, those who are poor are even more susceptible to hardships. Those who don't have secure employment can more easily lose it. Those who can't afford medication or vaccines can more easily get sick. These realities, side by side with how fast we could lose what we have ourselves, should keep us humble. Humility helps us understand our privileges and the supports we may have, like family or unemployment benefits, which can help us temporarily if something does go wrong.

While humility is one of the seven Attitudes of the Helping Heart explored in this book, our ability to develop the other six begins with our willingness to embrace a spirit of humility. We realize we are not better than anyone else, and this opens the door to caring for others.[8]

---

8 I thank Rev. Jim Lyon for the ideas in this paragraph.

Understanding Lack of Opportunities

Traveling and living abroad allows me to be even more aware of the privileges I have as an American citizen, something for which I'm grateful. People often tell me they dream of moving to the United States, of having a well-paying job. Living in the in-between of privilege and gratitude means I'm thankful for privileges I never earned. They are not given to me because of anything I did. So I remain uncomfortable with my comforts, recognizing not everyone has the same opportunities I have.

While I recognize privileges, like my nationality, are mine "just because," I also know they are given to me because of all who came before me, like soldiers who fought for my country and leaders who built a foundation for people to live in relative peace. This also includes slaves, taken from their homelands to serve people who, in some small or big way, supported the people who came before me. Ultimately, this means my privileges are connected to things I may very much oppose yet had no control over, such as innocent blood shed during atrocities that happened before I was even born, which paved the way for the development of my country as we know it. In short, I have what I have, in large part, because of all that happened long before I was alive. What I have didn't only come from my own two hands. It's deeply rooted in my many privileges. Recognizing that should keep me humble. It should keep us humble.

I've learned it helps to see my privileges on a split-screen, with them side by side with most of the world's population who doesn't have them.[9] Being a good steward of my privileges starts with acknowledging them—I have something very precious that others don't. Who I am and what I have is very much out of my control.

Similarly, the poverty of the poor is also very much out of their control. I need to understand my privileges for what they are and then balance that with an awareness of the lack of privileges of so many others, as what people don't have is often related to the privileges they don't have. They lack opportunities to rise above their poverty, keeping them from making ends meet. They're not able to fulfill the dreams they have for themselves and their families.

This is heartbreaking. It's like someone in a pit who dreams of getting out but can't, and it's not just one person, but millions. If it were just one, we'd think we could try to help, but with millions, we feel like giving up. To make matters worse, the pit is deep because of the conditions of the world. For most of the world's poor, no matter how much they want to get out of the pit of poverty, it's probably not possible. They were born into it, and they suffer from

---

9 I thank my former professor Diana Eck for introducing me to the split-screen way of thinking: "We are worried, and rightly so, about ISIS, about Ebola, about Ferguson … about the countless issues that are ours in a turbulent world, and maybe we can think about that possibility of the planet becoming uninhabitable somewhat later," she said. "But I would like to suggest that all of us, we and you alike, commit ourselves to retaining that split-screen world in which we hold our plans, our personal plans, our dreams, our abundant energies always and in juxtaposition with the images that disturb us and call us to everyday responsibility." Accessible at: https://news.harvard.edu/gazette/story/2014/12/getting-to-the-finish/.

everything that rages against them: a corrupt government; wars and violence; insufficient rain to water their crops; discrimination; lack of freedom, rights, and justice; and perhaps a history of people oppressing them, or stealing from them and killing them. These are hard things to overcome. It's not a pit from which one can easily escape.

And whether the poor are religious or not, or share the same faith as us or not, is irrelevant. Yet, we believe an individual's faith can be critical to helping them become all they can be. We'll soon read about the faith of Sak, Theary, and Pun. For many who are poor, while faith may help them in their struggle to get by in life, their individual faith is not likely to help them overcome their poverty, to get them out of the pit.

Using Our Privileges for a Greater Good

Many of us feel we should be doing more to help make the world a better place. We want to be responsible with what we've been given, doing good with what we have, doing our part to help those in need. But it's challenging to figure out how to use our privileges for a greater good.

I once heard a graduate of an elite university mention how he felt compelled to use his many privileges to benefit people in the world who are in need. This not only requires thinking beyond ourselves, but also transforming our natural state of self-centeredness into something that is more inclusive of other people. It requires challenging our future plans to ensure they're not entirely self-focused. That's rather inconvenient.

Writer and creator Jeff Goins once wrote in his email newsletter, "As a white man, I am acquainted with the invisible advantages that have benefited me my entire life. I have also learned that there is nothing noble about feeling guilty for this. It doesn't cost me anything to acknowledge my leg-ups in life, and doing so does not negate my hard work. But with these advantages come great responsibility. The point of my privilege is to acknowledge it so I can use it."[10]

How we utilize our privileges is one of life's greatest responsibilities. And we should consider our responsibilities humbly, remembering the situations in the world that disturb us, such as poverty, war, hunger, lack of clean water. The list goes on. Using our privileges for a greater good is like increasing their capacity. The more we use them to positively affect others, the greater their capacity to do good.

The Importance of Discomfort

In poor countries, many children who live or work on the streets pick through trash looking for recyclables, or find other ways to earn money. I first saw children picking through trash in India. Two boys stood in a parking lot, amidst a thirty-foot by thirty-foot collection of colorful litter thick enough to hide what was underneath it. Eight cows foraged next to them, looking for leftover food. The boys, about eight and ten years old, were collecting recyclables, working together to put the contents of one bag into the other. It was January, and they wore sweaters but didn't have gloves. One had earmuffs.

---

10   Email newsletter, June 17, 2020. Jeff Goins is found at http://www. goinswriter.com.

Similarly, in our neighborhood in Istanbul, young men from Afghanistan and Pakistan walk miles each day, dumpster to dumpster, looking for recyclables. They pull large carts, taller than they are and the size of a small car, made of canvas that was once white but is now gray and ragged. They make a few dollars each day and live together in shacks just to make ends meet. I heard some walk to Turkey through Iran. And I've read where others pay lots of money for their travel, believing they will find a decent job in Istanbul, the city where the glitzy soap operas they watch in their home countries are filmed. When they leave their families, they promise to send money back to them. But when they arrive, they can't find a job. They're trapped in a place they probably wished they'd never come to.

I often greet these men when I pass them on the street. And I do my small part to separate clean recyclables in our home, making their job easier and helping ensure our environmental impact is lessened. Most of us haven't had an experience where we're living in shacks and picking through dumpsters to salvage used plastic bottles and cardboard. We haven't had to sell the result of a hard day's labor for a few dollars, just to get by—and then get up and do it again and again.

When I look at these men, I'm often uncomfortable about the large gap between what I have and what they don't have—my privileges and their lack of privileges. Living in the in-between of gratitude and humility is, therefore, also a burden—one we should gladly accept in exchange for what we have. This burden should discomfort us. If we're in a place where we're not without, I think we should feel the burden of our privilege, feeling overwhelmed by what we have. In this way, discomfort is important. It shapes us into being the people we ought to be. It keeps us humble. It keeps us thankful. It keeps us aware of the magnitude of our world's problems.

Discomfort leads us to a place where we are bothered when we compare what we have to what others don't have. Discomfort reminds us that the material goods we have are greater than what most others have, and maybe even more than enough for us. This kind of discomfort helps us better live in the in-between of gratitude and humility, being thankful for what we have while also understanding we have it because of things that are out of our control. Does it really even all belong to us?

Feeling this burden of discomfort can also transform the way we think about what we have, even if it's just enough to scrape by each month. We become more grateful for what we have. We are more aware of those who are struggling. Living in the in-between of gratitude and humility helps us remember our privileges. It helps us fight the beast of resistance within us—self-centeredness, lack of generosity, and apathy—that causes us to forget those in need. We realize that since we have, we should therefore give.

Taking It to the Next Level

Review the reflective questions, recite the prayer, read the Bible passage, take the challenge, and write your personal reflections in the free *7 Attitudes of the Helping Heart Companion Study Guide*.

Download the free study guide at:
http://www.johnchristopherframe.org

In the Words of Sak, the Security Guard

Reflections on life as a Buddhist monk

I am Buddhist and I used to be a monk. I was a monk for nearly two years. I wore the dark-yellow robes, and my head was shaved. I lived in the pagoda in my village, near my house. About seven or eight of us monks lived at the pagoda. We would walk around to people's homes to collect food and money.

When you start as a monk, it's normal to feel shy about that, going from house to house. When we go and people give us rice, for example, it is like they are doing a good deed for us. But, actually, it is giving people an opportunity to gain merit for their next life. By giving to us, they're doing good deeds for their next life. We are actually helping them. When they give rice to us, we give words to bless them—that they may live in peace and happiness. It's like a blessing.

Life as a monk includes things like cutting wood in the mornings, cleaning the area around the pagoda, and cutting the grass. I liked to grow vegetables and flowers in the garden at the pagoda.

We'd spend a lot of time memorizing our chanting script. When we were invited to go to a special event to chant, we didn't want to be embarrassed because we didn't know the script. Normally, I got up around 3:00 to 4:00 a.m. and would go to bed around 11:00 to 12:00 at night. Sometimes

I was really focused on studying the script, and I'd stay up until 1:00 a.m.

In the afternoons, we would rest. Normally, monks eat only two times a day. That is the rule. They can eat in the morning and have an early lunch. In the evening they can't eat, but they can drink water and juice. So the time for not eating is from noon until the next morning, around 6:00 a.m.

I have an eagle tattoo. Most monks have a tattoo of a dragon or an eagle, or some other powerful animal—it's like a power that helps them. And when other people see the tattoo, they are afraid of that power. So my tattoo is not a tattoo that people would normally have. It is a special one. It's like a sign of protection. When you have this kind of symbol, you need to eliminate some kind of food or activity from your life forever. I chose an eagle because an eagle is a kind of bird that other birds are afraid of. And, of course, it can fly.

In the Words of Theary, the Garment Factory Worker

Reflections on personal faith

I've been a Christian since 2008. I was Buddhist before. My dad is a Christian now too. He goes to church every Sunday.

There was someone who was handing out tracts about Christianity in front of the garment factory. I just took it and dropped it on the street. Later on, I received one again and I read it. The person who gave it to me talked to me.

After I heard preaching at the church, I could feel the difference between Christianity and Buddhism—I could feel the difference in my life. Now I serve as an elder in the church, and I take some people to our small groups with my motorbike.

In the Words of Pun, the Great-Grandmother

Reflections on starting the church

*M*y village is very safe. There's not any crime, though there were some wars during and after the Khmer Rouge. Even so, I wasn't afraid then, even though there were guns and some bombs, because my husband used to have this little magical thing he wore. It was my husband's and kids' thing; I didn't do anything with it myself. But we believed it had spiritual or magical power and that it would protect us. Like I never got sick or anything. In the past, before I believed in Jesus, I believed in those spirits—that they kept us safe—but now I don't. I don't really know if anyone around here still believes in that magic. No one really talks about it anymore.

I don't remember when I became a Christian, but it was more than twenty years ago. I learned about Jesus from my sister in Australia, and from some foreigners. My sister asked me to be on the lookout for some land in the village to buy. When I was younger and full of energy, I liked building up things, like getting the community together for a gathering, and we created the church here. My sister brought along some foreigners and some people from Phnom Penh to join us for a while when we were building the church. We would have some meals together and it was fun. Before that, there wasn't any church here.

At first, the church was made up of only my family. Then we tried to spread the word in the village. There were a lot of believers, but some left for various reasons. But there are new people who are coming and becoming Christians, so it increases.

I told people about Jesus, but some only thought about getting money. Some would fake being Christian to get supported, like for their own personal benefit. When they got what they wanted, they left and stopped believing in Jesus. Despite that, there are some good people who believe in Jesus and are always willing to contribute to the church.

Because I'm old, some people ask me why I'm trying to work and contribute to the church. They say I won't get anything out of it, but I don't care what they say.

Chapter 4

Empathy: Embracing the Power of Co-Suffering

When I was born, a man named Pol Pot was leading a radical communist revolution, the Khmer Rouge, nine thousand miles away, in Cambodia. Communist soldiers with large guns kicked families out of their homes in the city, and forced them into the countryside to dig canals and plant crops as slaves.

The government was everyone's overseer. Doctors and teachers were murdered. Religious leaders were killed, along with people who wore eyeglasses and others thought to be elite. Money was abolished. Books were burned. Religious practices were banned. Victims were taken from their families and hit on the head with metal tools, then tossed into mass graves. Children were beaten to death. Though it's impossible to know for sure, some say about 2 million people died from starvation, disease, and execution during the years of the Khmer Rouge. Mothers, babies, grandparents, everyone, were victims of unthinkable atrocities. It was one of the world's worst genocides.

When my wife and I lived in Cambodia, we visited an old high-school-turned-execution-compound, now a museum, where black-and-white photos of victims gaze back at visitors. Torture devices are displayed, and nets of rusty barbed wire still enclose the outdoor corridors.

We also visited one of the "Killing Fields," now memorial grounds where clothing sometimes surfaces from mass graves. There is a tall monument with stacks of human skulls looking out over the grounds, as if they are mourning the dead. While walking around, we passed a glass box the size of a large aquarium, full of fragments of human bones. Another was filled with victims' clothes. On top of that box were remnants visitors had found on the ground and added to the collection: the bottom of a flip-flop, several teeth. Around some of the mass graves were waist-high bamboo fences where visitors had left hundreds of colorful hand-made bracelets, one with a small cross.

A sign next to a large tree stated it had been used to hang a loud speaker that covered over the moans of the victims being executed. Another sign named a different tree the "killing tree." A painting inside the small museum there showed a militant holding a baby by the legs, the mother being dragged away while reaching for it.

Trauma from catastrophes like the Khmer Rouge does not easily go away. It doesn't only affect the generation that lived through it. Post-traumatic stress disorder can haunt survivors of trauma so much that it affects their offspring.[11] Scientists have explored how trauma is passed down genetically to later generations.[12]

Sadly, the Khmer Rouge somehow affects everyone in Cambodia even today. As we'll soon learn, Sak's father was killed, and several of Pun's children died. To this day, the terror of the Khmer Rouge continues to bring suffering on the country.

Understanding Suffering

Suffering seems normal in our world. Unfortunately, it's too common. The world is full of suffering and it always has been. War and other atrocities, extensive poverty, lack of freedom, political tyrants, and earthquakes and other natural disasters are all things we hear about regularly. We're accustomed to bad news.

While we know suffering exists, I think those of us who live in relative comfort may find it difficult to really understand the pain others go through. Maybe it's even impossible. When suffering hits close to home, we have no choice but to endure it. But if we don't suffer from extreme poverty, natural disasters, preventable disease, or lack of food and

---

11 Judith Shulevitz, "The Science of Suffering," *The New Republic*, November 16, 2014, https://newrepublic.com/article/120144/trauma-genetic-scientists-say-parents-are-passing-ptsd-kids.

12 Virginia Hughes, "Sperm RNA carries marks of trauma," *Nature*, April 17, 2014, https://www.nature.com/news/polopoly_fs/1.15049!/menu/main/topColumns/topLeftColumn/pdf/508296a.pdf.

clean water, we may go on with our days forgetting about those experiencing these things. Yet, even though we may not suffer from these types of burdens, we may suffer from other things going on in life.

There are different types and degrees of suffering. Some people suffer from illness, others from injustice, poverty, or anxiety about the past or future. Sometimes, suffering jolts us from a peaceful sleep. Some of us wake up with physical pain. Others awake and quickly remember something sad. Some of us can't sleep at all. And while our own personal suffering may be small compared to that of others, it's still suffering. In one way or another, it's something we all face at some point.

While our own times of suffering can allow us to reconnect with God—to trust God to pull us through—the experience can be excruciating. When we suffer, we can't think straight, always weighed down by whatever is bothering us. We pray for God's help and mercy. When we suffer, no matter what it's about, we feel it at our core.

I sometimes make the mistake of downplaying the suffering of those of us who live relatively comfortable lives. For example, in the past, when my wife experienced some difficulty in life, my strategy was to help her see reality as I saw it. "The problems you have aren't really problems," I'd tell her. "There are people who would love to trade their problems for yours."

My approach seemed reasonable. I was trying to get her to quickly snap out of the feelings she was having. But suffering isn't like that. Through her tears, she'd look at me and say, "It doesn't matter how small my problems are. They're still real problems. Everyone's problems are big to them."

Through these conversations, my wife taught me that suffering is suffering, regardless of what it's about, and no matter how small it may seem to an outsider. Through her, I learned no suffering is trivial, and that I should never downplay it, no matter how "small" it may seem.

What Is Co-Suffering?

Helping others often begins with empathizing with them, feeling their pain. So why is it so difficult for us to feel the suffering of others? It may be because we only look at ourselves when we suffer.

When I suffer, it's something for me to feel. When others suffer, it's something for them to experience. However, what I've come to realize is that my own personal suffering can remind me of the difficulties others experience. My own moments of suffering can allow me to better understand I'm not alone in my suffering. This is co-suffering.

Empathy has always been a challenge for me, but one afternoon, when I wasn't expecting it at all, I had a profound experience of deep empathy. It happened at a fitness club in London. That day, I planned to indulge at the club's spa, really getting my money's worth of the membership fee. At some point, I entered the sanarium—a not-too-hot-sauna where you can relax and forget about everything on the outside. It is quiet and warm, with a soft smell of cedar wood and dimmed lights. It was a haven all to myself.

At that time in my life, a couple of small things were causing me to suffer. Not the kind of emotional pain that haunted me, keeping me from doing anything else, but the kind that nagged me when I awoke, or maybe even in the middle of the night. The kind that stopped me from having peace. The kind that made me feel blah in my stomach when I thought about it. My wife was also experiencing some suffering at that time. Regardless of how small these issues were compared to the problems of others, they were still troubling.

That afternoon in the sanarium, I prayed for my wife, feeling the burden of her suffering and probably that of my own. I began to cry. Then a strange thing happened. A few images and thoughts of suffering people around the world came to my mind. The most distinct image was that of a young man in Indonesia whose wife had been washed away in the recent tsunami. Though I'll never know if the man actually existed, he was standing outside alone, his home and life destroyed. Other thoughts and images flashed through my mind, staying on one before moving to another. My crying developed into a long period of weeping. I thought of God suffering with these individuals.

When I suffer personally or cry, I feel almost spiritually transported to a place where my soul feels more connected to God. But in the stillness and solitude of that sanarium, I felt something more—a type of empathy I'd never experienced before. In my own suffering, I had a glimpse, in some small way, of the suffering of others. Despite the vast differences between what I was going through and what those I envisioned were going through, I felt my own suffering was positioning me to co-suffer with them. Of course, it was a temporary experience, and my suffering could never be compared to theirs. I don't know the pain of those I wept for. I didn't feel the same suffering they did. Despite that, I feel I was empathizing with them, miles away.

My experience that day led me to think about how personal suffering can allow us to be co-sufferers with others. Our own suffering can remind us of the pain others are going through, even if it's different from our own. When we suffer, we remember others are suffering too. We remember we're not alone.

In the book *Tuesdays with Morrie*, Mitch Albom relays the words of his professor, Morrie Schwartz, dying from Lou Gehrig's disease. Morrie states, "Now that I'm suffering, I feel closer to people who suffer than I ever did before." He described how he'd seen on television people running in Bosnia, afraid of getting hit by gunfire. He said, "I just started to cry. I feel their anguish as if it were my own."[13] Because of his own illness, he was feeling the suffering of people thousands of miles away. That is co-suffering.

Co-suffering is about empathizing with others. It's sharing in the act of suffering. In my suffering, I suffer with you. In your suffering, you suffer with me. It's a way to remember that we're with each other through difficult times. And God is with us as well.

My membership to that fitness club expired a few days later and I never returned. Even so, that experience taught

---

13 Mitch Albom, *Tuesdays with Morrie: an old man, a young man, and life's greatest lesson* (New York: Doubleday, 1997), 50.

me about how personal suffering, even temporary, can lead us to think about others going through difficulties. Just as I think more about those with chronic pain when I have some kind of temporary physical pain myself, through our own suffering, we can begin to feel the suffering of others. As different as our suffering may be, we can co-suffer with them.

I would not have had that co-suffering experience that afternoon had I not been experiencing suffering myself, though it was temporary and very different than the suffering of those who flashed through my mind. And I wouldn't have been suffering as much personally if I hadn't also been feeling my wife's suffering. It was all connected.

Empathy: A First Step

How can we better empathize with those who are suffering?

In a world where we usually focus on ourselves, our family, and our friends, feeling the suffering of people we don't know might take work. Without being intentional, we may not be able to feel empathy.

When we relate to others, in person or in spirit, we position ourselves to share in their suffering. Finding ways of becoming more aware of suffering in the world and in our local communities can help us better tune in to it. This can be through connecting with nonprofits and faith-based organizations, which can offer us ways of learning about and empathizing with those in need. Documentaries and online videos can expose us to the problems of people we'll never have a chance to meet. Intentionally learning about people and their problems increases our ability to empathize and co-suffer with them, even if we don't know how to really help them.

It's okay not to know what to do when information about world atrocities overwhelm us. We're not heroes. We're co-sufferers. Empathizing with others is one small step in living out our faith and caring for those in need. But it's not enough.

It is true that empathy won't stop droughts that make poor people poorer. It won't stop people feeling they need to sell their bodies because they can't find other ways of earning an income. It won't stop corrupt leaders who harm their country politically and economically. However, it can at least make us better people—ones more emotionally connected with and concerned about the suffering of others. It is an important Attitude of the Helping Heart, as empathy can lead us further on our journey of helping those in need.

The truth is, on our own, we probably won't know how to deal with the world's problems. As Christians and people who want to do good, we may not know how to truly help. We may not think we have the ability. Nevertheless, we can begin asking ourselves and each other, "What can—or should—I do to help?"

Through empathizing with others, we can begin to get clarity about what roles we *can* play to make the world a better place. Empathy is critical to having a helping heart.

Taking It to the Next Level

Review the reflective questions, recite the prayer, read the Bible passage, take the challenge, and write your personal reflections in the free *7 Attitudes of the Helping Heart Companion Study Guide.*

Download the free study guide at:
http://www.johnchristopherframe.org

In the Words of Sak, the Security Guard

Reflections on losing a parent in war

*B*efore I was born, my parents went through the Khmer Rouge regime. All of my father's siblings passed away during the Khmer Rouge. And my father's parents—my grandparents—were killed.

My father was also killed when I was sixteen. He was a soldier and he died next to the border of Thailand, when he was in the service. At that time, there was still a war between the Cambodian government and the Khmer Rouge. My father died in the fighting. He was killed by the Khmer Rouge, as some parts of the country were still controlled by them. He was on the government's side.

My dad's closest friend came to tell us. He used to come and eat meals at our home. He said my dad had stepped on a mine and got injured on his feet. Then the Khmer Rouge burned the forest where he was, and he couldn't get out. I think he died because of the fire. He had run out of luck. When my mother heard this news, she cried and cried and rolled around in the dirt. She cried for days, and started drinking.

My father was skilled, and he built our house. There weren't any rooms inside, just one big room. One side of the house was wood and the other parts were cloth. The roof was tile. My dad couldn't finish the house before he died, but my *sister saved up and borrowed money to finish it. My mother still lives there, and it has electricity now. The house isn't on stilts, so the rain used to come and flood the house, but then we worked on the land so that wouldn't happen. Our whole family lived in that house.*

After my father died, I couldn't focus anymore. I was distracted and couldn't study, and I dropped out of school.

In the words of Pun, the Great-Grandmother

Reflections on the Khmer Rouge

*B*ack before the Khmer Rouge, we were all well off. During the Khmer Rouge, I was selected to be a Khmer Rouge team leader. It's like a commander. I was assigned to a small group. During that period, I saw how people would exchange their gold for rice. That's how hungry they were. My son was selected to be a Khmer Rouge soldier. They took him and ordered him to be in Pol Pot's militia. He was eighteen. We had no choice even though we didn't want to be part of it. Whenever I talk about that time period, I really miss him.

I gave birth to twelve children. In addition to my son who died in the militia, three of my other children also died during the time of the Khmer Rouge. In total, seven of my children have passed away. The youngest five are alive. I believe it was destiny—they had to go, even before me, their own mother. Death is normal, people live and die. It's the cycle of life.

I felt close to God during those times. God helped me through it and guided me to keep on living, and I want to serve God back. God is in my heart and mind—like a shelter I can always seek.

Chapter 5

Compassion: Starting Near and Spreading Far

In India, children and their parents work side by side making bricks. They live in small shacks about the size of a prison cell, with ceilings so low the parents can't stand up straight inside. After they arrive to begin working at the brick kiln, their first project is making the bricks they use to build their "homes."

When the children are old enough to walk, they help with cleaning. Older children look after younger siblings. By the time they are eight years old, they've joined their parents making bricks. These families work ten-hour days in extreme heat, dust, and smoke. The flames in the kilns are so hot they've been described as hellfire. The closest thing to hell on earth, I've been told. The families work with nothing to really protect themselves. They usually walk around in bare feet, sometimes wearing flip-flops.

While the families get a break during the rainy season, they return later to continue working. In some kilns, they return to find that the kiln owners have torn down their homes to sell the bricks, forcing the families to make new bricks and build again. Many of the families are recruited from poorer parts of India, a long journey from the kilns. Although promised good wages, they're indebted to their employers and only paid a little over $6.00 per one thousand bricks they make. The families are under generational debt bondage, owing money they'll never be able to repay.

In a small number of these brick kilns, Catholic sisters have been given an open door to visit the families. The Arise Foundation, a secular organization that supports the work of these sisters, reported that most of the families suffer from malnutrition, with their diet consisting only of rice and lentils. The sisters, along with some locals they've hired to assist them, teach the children basic literacy and how to count. They use walls of bricks as chalkboards, and organize activities and games. They bring them toys so they can feel like kids at least for a little while each day.

The sisters support the families in other ways as well. They organize health services and trainings on basic hygiene and life skills. They conduct educational classes for adults to improve their literacy and teach them about their rights. They've even helped the families develop a way to pool their money to cover emergencies, creating something like an informal credit union, thus reducing their need to use loan sharks.

The brick kiln owners were suspicious of the sisters, as they didn't want the families to run away or turn against them, but the owners permitted them to enter after the sisters effectively wore them down, making regular visits and requests for permission to help. They were finally told yes because they were sisters, which speaks to the value of persistence as well as the uniqueness of their status. Other groups would have been refused.

The work of Catholic sisters in India expands far beyond what they do in those brick kilns, including providing services that help to *prevent* human trafficking and modern slavery. Luke de Pulford, Director of the Arise Foundation, states that sisters provide unconditional loving accompaniment. In other words, they are with people, just because. It takes a lot of time, and they are excellent at it, he said.

The sisters love and value the people they help. They've fully committed themselves to serving God and the needs of others. Most of us, however, have not committed our lives to full-time charity work. We don't live near the world's most-exploited people. Yet, we can still learn something about compassion from the work of these sisters that can help us on our own journey of caring about those in need. Empathy, discussed in the previous chapter, is something internal. Compassion is outward facing. It's related not only to how we feel but what we do.

In order to want to help people in poverty, we need to care about them. Even if we don't yet have the knowledge of how to help, we can have it in our hearts to care.

Caring for People We Know and Don't Know

People in need come from all backgrounds and religions, just like everybody. What does it look like to care about people who are different from us and have needs we really can't fathom? How can we care about people we don't know? I think it starts with caring for people we already know.

When my wife and I lived in London, we stayed in a traditional rowhouse, where each home in a block is attached to the one next to it. Each was two stories, with one unit on the bottom and a separate one above. Tall fences separated small gardens in the back. I occasionally spoke with the neighbor downstairs whose garden was next to ours. Our other neighbors, to the left, were from Pakistan. When they moved in, the man brought over a box of chocolates and apologized in advance for the noise we'd be hearing from his children.

Typically, in British culture, people tend to keep to themselves, exchanging kind greetings with strangers or acquaintances as necessary. Politeness and privacy are closely related. Especially in London, people are busy with family and work and a social life planned weeks and months in advance.

Next door to us lived a man and his adult daughter. Though most of our walls touched each other, the houses were built so, when we looked out our kitchen window, we could look into the window of their kitchen, about twenty feet away. The man always kept his window shade down partway so that when he stood at his kitchen sink, our eyes wouldn't have to meet. One time, as he started to pull the shade down, my wife caught his eyes, smiled, and waved. He waved back and didn't pull the shade down as far that time. We never met him, but my wife had occasionally spoken to his daughter on the sidewalk. Sometimes they'd wave to each other from one kitchen window to the other.

One Saturday afternoon, a police car was parked on the street outside of our home. It stayed there for hours. Then an ambulance arrived and, after that, a large black van with no windows. We looked from our kitchen window and could see a police officer standing inside our neighbor's kitchen. I looked from another window to watch from a different angle. First, there was one officer looking at the floor. Then there was another. It seemed like they were looking at a body, one standing near the head, the other at the feet. I asked my wife if she thought it was a murder.

Later, two men carried out a body bag and put it in the black van. As the police were getting into their car to leave, my wife asked them what happened. "You can ask the daughter when she comes home. I'm afraid I can't say," one officer responded.

For a long time, my wife didn't like to go into the kitchen anymore. I was also feeling a burden, wondering if the man had taken his own life. We later learned that our neighbor had committed suicide, something he'd been talking about for years, his daughter told my wife over coffee at a local café. He had instabilities in his mental health, she said.

The day he died, I had been sitting on the couch, just on the other side of his wall. Yet, I had no thoughts about him. I never even knew his name. I probably had seen his face only once—and it was only from a glance, of course, before he pulled down his window shade.

When my wife and I lived in the UK, a suicide prevention campaign, #SmallTalkSavesLives, encouraged people to look around for those who might seem troubled, especially in train stations. It's estimated that for every life lost by suicide on the railway, six are saved by people around them.[14] *You have all the experience you need to help save a life*, the campaign told us. Ads encouraged people to garner confidence to initiate small talk with people who looked troubled. Engaging a person contemplating suicide, even about the weather, is often enough to prevent them from doing it, we were told.

I often have pondered, *What is my responsibility for my next-door neighbors in need? How about my responsibility for those who don't live next door? For those I never meet at all?*

College Freshmen Sharing Compassion

My first job teaching in a college classroom was a part-time role teaching two critical thinking classes for college freshmen. I engaged students in reflective questions about life. Together we explored important works from authors like Brontë, Bourdieux, and C. S. Lewis.

One weekend, some seniors at the university who lived off campus hosted a bonfire and I was invited. At the bonfire

---

14 See https://www.samaritans.org/support-us/campaign/small-talk-saves-lives/ and https://www.youtube.com/watch?v=VDchxgZxjcM.

was a student who I knew from the group of freshmen that drove to downtown Indianapolis to visit with the homeless every Friday evening. They'd pool their money together and buy pizzas and burgers. Homeless people would gather and wait for their arrival each week, as if they were going to a party. The students would arrive, share the food they'd bought, and hang around and talk.

At the bonfire, I spoke with this freshman about his work with the homeless. Taking too seriously my role as a college instructor, I challenged him, as the devil's advocate, with pointed questions and comments that I thought would help him think more critically about the impact he and his friends were having. "Is what you're doing bringing about change in the lives of the homeless?" I asked. "Do you really think you're helping them?"

I failed to recall that Jesus, when he fed the five thousand, wasn't worried about changing those people or even stopping their future hunger. For some reason, my attitude was wrong when I was speaking with this student. I acted prideful and all-knowing. I was the teacher and he was the freshman, though not a student in my class. I was taking my passion for critical thinking and spinning it into something that was condescending. The student's face changed, as what I'd said seemed to have squashed his spirit. I worried I had extinguished his passion, his belief in the value of caring for the homeless through presence. And that was wrong.

At some point that night, a spark popped from the bonfire, landing on my favorite shirt and burning a little hole in it, as if I were receiving a small punishment in advance for overanalyzing and belittling the caring actions of others. This student and his friends were thoughtful and generous. I was judgmental and haughty. Their aim was to share friendship and food. They did that well. I saw it myself.

When I joined them once on a Friday night, I remember meeting a fifty-something homeless man, Tim, wearing a baseball cap and worn clothes, and holding a brown cardboard sign that read *Got Milk?* Tim had recently changed bridges he stayed under, he said, after teenagers stormed their former encampment with baseball bats. He talked about having grown up in a Christian family and wanting to become a minister someday. He loved to read and enjoyed the books one of the students regularly gave him.

I'm sure the kindness of these students brought some type of change in the lives of the homeless people they met each week. It had to have. What they did was remarkable, caring for the homeless and spending their money on them week after week. Their presence was a beautiful example of being compassionate to those in need. A few weeks later, I spoke to the student I'd talked to at the bonfire about how he felt after our conversation. I still fear that I had a negative impact on him, though, and have prayed for him a number of times since.

The next year, when continuing my education at Harvard, I chose to join the Street Team of the Harvard Square Homeless Shelter as part of a course requirement to be involved in something to learn about poverty in the real world. I had a shift once a week, walking around with a couple of other students, saying hello and checking in with people who were homeless in the business district bordering the university. It was one of the ways I was introduced to the streets that I'd spend much more time on the following summer, sharing life with the homeless community, as captured in my first book, *Homeless at Harvard: Finding Faith and Friendship on the Streets of Harvard Square.*

As members of the Street Team, we'd offer hats and gloves and would give out hot food. It wasn't quite the pizza parties the freshmen organized in Indianapolis, and we didn't pay for it out of our own pockets. However, our check-ins were meaningful to the homeless people we met. It was even more meaningful to me, I think. It gave me a small purpose—a chance to feel I was doing something—and it was an opportunity to talk to people on the streets, learning about something I knew very little about. It also provided me a way to connect with other students and make new friends.

As a street team, our actions seemed to be helping us just as much as, if not more than, those we met. That's what's interesting about compassion. The more you give, the more you might receive something in return. The more you serve, the better you might feel. The more you help others, the more you might help yourself.

The Importance of Small Acts of Caring

Caring for others isn't necessarily easy. But we can all start somewhere.

Having compassion for others comes from thinking about people and doing something practical, even something small. This may be saying hello to someone you pass on the sidewalk or offering a homeless person a pair of new socks. It may be sharing in a prayer group about something you learned that happened overseas that upset you.

Compassion is demonstrated in small everyday acts, like showing people you value them, especially those whom others may not treat well, like a low-paid employee at a place you do business. It's looking that person in the eye and telling them they're doing a good job. Step by step, compassion and acts of caring can grow; it begins with first putting your feelings into action.

While small acts of thoughtfulness may seem minor to us, what if your hello changed the outcome of someone's day? What if your kindness helped a person have a clearer mind? What if it encouraged someone to make a better decision, like keeping a job instead of becoming unemployed? What if it helped someone to interact better with their children? What if your simple acts of caring were that powerful?

They can be. Small actions may not be small at all. As mentioned above, small talk can even save a life.

Small acts of caring go a long way in helping and encouraging people in ways we'll never know. They also help us. Sharing kindness can make us happier people, and it helps fight the beast of resistance within us.

But what if the person you speak to doesn't say anything back or seems annoyed at you? Think of your words as a small gift with nothing expected in return. The person you speak to probably feels at least a little better on the inside even if it doesn't show on the outside.

In *Homeless at Harvard*, I wrote about how people helped those living on the streets in small ways. A retired man, rumored to be a proctologist, passed out Fig Newtons. Women walking to work chatted with a homeless man who sold newspapers. Volunteers of the Outdoor Church toted around coolers containing sandwiches that they gave out. These acts of caring made a difference. People were doing something to try to help. Putting actions to our feelings in everyday settings prepares us for helping people in other ways in the future, including people who live far away we'll never get to meet.

So how can we care about people in such a way that we impact them?

Sometimes I find myself very jovial. I'll say hello to strangers. I'll think about how other people feel. I'll give attention to people whom others may dismiss, ensuring they know I see them or value their work, that they're important enough to talk to. I'll be that vessel of God's love I want to be.

Other times, though, I'm not that way. I keep to myself. I don't feel God's Spirit moving through me. And that's not a good place to be. Sometimes I feel a burden for people living in poverty. Other times I don't, or that burden is lighter than it should be. What I've realized is that when my own heart is far from God, I don't feel compassion for others in the way I should. My sin overshadows the love in my heart for others, resulting in less kindness, less compassion, less of everything good that comes from God's Spirit. This is critical to understand and something I discuss further in the next chapter, as our relationship with God is integral to our being compelled to care for those in need.

When my heart feels clean, I feel more in sync with God and the world around me. It's in these times that it's easier to interact with people in a way that expresses compassion. I can feel more like a conduit of God's love, interacting with people out of the peace and joy in my own life. That's what it comes down to, I think: peace and joy in our soul from living a life that is pleasing to God. This results in having more compassion for others and sharing it outwardly. It allows us to more fully express to others this important Attitude of the Helping Heart.

Theology of Relational Care

Christians helping out of a responsibility to their faith, by putting action to their compassion and connecting with people in a way that demonstrates kindness, relates to what I call a theology of relational care. Specifically, this is a way of thinking about the ideas and actions related to connecting with people in need, and building relationships with them, whenever we can, especially those who feel excluded in our communities.

In terms of those who are severely economically poor, however, most live far away. We'll never have the chance to meet them, like mothers around the world who are losing their children to preventable diseases. We really can't practice a theology of relational care in terms of befriending these people. In addition, they may not be socially excluded. They may have family and friends, but they're still poor and in need. They need their problems solved more than they need relationships with people in other countries.

Taking Action

Caring for people living in poverty, whether we know them or not, is most easily accomplished when we feel connected to their problems and needs. This starts with recognizing the thing within us that wants to block out sad stories and bad news—the thought that poor people are going to get through it, just like we all get through it, whether or not we really care. The real difficulty we face in helping those in need is fighting the beast of resistance within us that stops us from helping and caring about others—the thing that stops us from acting on our awareness that many people are in need of something we may be able to share. For some, that may be sharing a kind word. For others, it is money or something tangible.

As humans, most of us are naturally self-centered. We think about ourselves and those close to us before we think of strangers. We think about the money in our own pockets before the money in someone else's. We buy things for ourselves before we buy them for others. This isn't necessarily bad. It's natural. Yet, it's something worth thinking about, this self-centeredness.

There is a battle within many of us—a fight within ourselves against the beast of resistance—as we weigh our wants and needs against the needs of others. This beast of resistance attacks us when we think about taking action to help others, such as when we're deciding how much to give to charity. Effective compassion requires we acknowledge this battle, to fight the beast of resistance. Recognizing it—even talking about it—can help us reflect on how we can best care for those in need, whether they need emotional support and friendship, or something else.

In order to help those who are poor, we need to have an attitude that desires to help. We may not do that well. We may not even know how to do it; nevertheless, caring is about matching action with our feelings. We also need to actually know about the needs of those living in poverty. We need to know about the problems they face, as this leads us to developing compassion and thinking intelligently about how to help. To do this, we must understand those in need, read about world problems, and learn about effective charities, much the same as we need to do when we want to develop greater empathy, discussed in the previous chapter.

Furthermore, while doing something is better than doing nothing, we should balance the feeling that we're helping with another realization: what we're doing is probably not enough. This should lead us to become wiser about how we can help and the best ways to do it. This means we need to get smarter. Smarter about how to give, how much to give, and to whom. Smarter about where our money goes, who it helps, and how.

It is critically important to consider what our actions—money, kindness, or otherwise—will do for others. This is especially the case with donating money. Think of it like this: just like we prefer to buy groceries on sale so we get more "bang for our buck," we should also consider the "bang for our buck" our donations have.

The Life You Can Save, an organization that promotes high-impact giving to effective charities, states it's not a strong sense of compassion that should determine where we donate. Instead, they say, "The most cost-effective, greatest impact giving requires both compassion and careful analysis: the Head and the Heart."[15] What this means is that not only should we learn about the needs of others and care about them, but we should also learn about the organizations that help them so we can make informed decisions to help the most people in the best ways.

Many people who are in desperate need will never ask us personally for anything. This especially includes those who live far away who we'll never meet. Being compassionate, then, means being aware of the needs of others, wherever they live in the world, *and* taking action to respond to those needs. This is compassion, rooted in love.

Taking It to the Next Level

Review the reflective questions, recite the prayer, read the Bible passage, take the challenge, and write your personal reflections in the free *7 Attitudes of the Helping Heart Companion Study Guide.*

Download the free study guide at:
http://www.johnchristopherframe.org

---

15   The Life You Can Save - Email newsletter, May 28, 2020.

In the Words of Theary,
the Garment Factory Worker

Reflections on work

*O*n my first day on the job in the garment factory, the leader told me to do a lot of things, and I wanted to quit. But I couldn't quit because of my financial problem; I had to try hard. I was told to clean the floor and dust and move clothes from one place to another.

My job was, and still is, in the quality control department, inspecting the clothes before they leave the factory to make sure there are no flaws in them. If I find any mistake, I have to send them back to the seamstresses.

I inspect an average of five hundred articles of clothing every day. If it is a simple design, the inspection takes less than a minute, but more complex designs take longer.

All of us at the factory have a team leader. Sometimes this leader is really strict. On the other hand, some leaders allow their employees to take a rest. The team leader just pretends not to see it. But if a non-Cambodian manager comes by, they will talk to the workers and leader about why they're resting.

I have a good relationship with my team leader sometimes, if there is no problem with the clothes. But when there is a problem, then he always gets upset. Sometimes our team leader just does things to please the boss. He'll *give us a list and we'll follow it, but if there's a problem, he won't take responsibility. "The workers made the mistake," he'll say.*

Most workers in the factory are women, but men work there too. The factory doesn't like to recruit older people because if there is some problem, they will complain to the managers and advocate for themselves. If the factory recruits young people, it is easier for the managers. The young people will just do what they say.

The youngest girl I met in the factory was about thirteen to fourteen years old. There are a lot of underage people in the factory. When the government comes to monitor the factory, the boss tells those who are under eighteen not to come to work that day. I don't think the owners of the factory should hire underage people.

There are two working shifts in the factory: from morning to evening, 7 a.m. to 6 p.m., and evening to morning, 7 p.m. to 6 a.m. I work Monday through Saturday on the day shift. Overtime is 6 p.m. to 8:30 p.m. Monday through Friday. For me, I only do overtime sometimes, when they need it. In the sewing department, some people work overtime every day. I have most Sundays off, but sometimes I work then, if there is a need.

The workers who sew get higher pay than me because they get paid based on the number of pieces they make. So, if they make a lot of clothes, they get paid more money. For me, though, I have a fixed salary. If I want more salary, I have to work overtime or holidays. My salary is about $120 to $130 per month. If I don't work Sundays or overtime, I just make $90 per month.[16]

Employees don't have much freedom. The boss needs all the workers to work overtime. Even if the employees don't want to, they have to do it. Some employees get sick and ask permission to go home or to rest, but the factory doesn't allow it. The boss forces the employees to work, and they work without any freedom. This is mostly with the people who sew rather than us in quality control. For the seamstresses, when the demand is high, they have to keep working.

If the boss wants the workers to work but they leave, the next day they'll get a warning from the office. If they do it again, they'll get fired. So, most of the time, overtime is not a choice for the workers.

I've worked in three garment factories doing the same job. In the first factory, there were about six thousand workers. In the second and third factories, there were about one thousand workers each. Nowadays, if you want to start working at the factory, they ask if you have any experience. If you don't have experience or any knowledge about making clothes, you have to give money to the recruiter in order to get the job. It's like corruption. Many factories have that problem now. You'll get two options. If you have the money now, you can pay it now. If you don't, then you have to pay it after you get your salary. It's about $30 to $35. If you have experience, then you don't have to pay.

---

16 The minimum wage in Cambodia has increased in recent years, since my interview with Theary. It still remains below what many feel is an adequate amount.

When the factory recruits employees, they say the salary is a certain amount, but when you go to work, you don't actually get that much. They'll say, "You came late, your working quality is low, so you can't get the salary we had posted." What is announced and what is reality is different.

Chapter 6

Generosity and Holiness: Being All God Wants You to Be

I've never thought of myself as a generous person, and I don't like that. Sometimes I think I'm generous, like when I leave a small tip for the cleaner at a hotel. But then I learn later that other customers gave much more.

When I'm generous, I admit, I feel a bit self-important. The day my wife and I moved back to Istanbul from London, I ate at a café and left a tip the waiter actually appreciated. Though it was small, when I considered its value converted to British pounds, it seemed like a good tip. I felt a little proud about it. When I returned to that café later, the waiter welcomed me with a smile, walked me to my table, and helped me with the chair as if I were an important figure. I felt honored, like a person who does good deeds. I felt generous, like I had plenty and that leaving a good tip was something normal for me. That made me feel good.

On that next visit to the café, though, I wondered how I could give a tip that was a little smaller than the first. *I won't order dessert this time so my bill won't be as high,* I thought. *I probably tipped more than other customers anyway.* It was as if the beast of resistance was creeping into my mind again, just when generosity was beginning to prevail. But then again, maybe the amount I had previously left wasn't generous at all, and the waiter was kind to me simply because he was a nice person.

I've begun to reflect that I shouldn't compare my generosity to others'. Instead of comparing what I give to what others give, I should compare what I have with what others don't have. Even though some people give little or nothing, I should give in a way that reflects my ability to share with others the gifts I've been given. My giving should be a reflection of what I have, where my heart is, and the value I see in others.

Relational Generosity

Generosity is about more than giving money. It includes how we understand people. As people who are generous, we see people as created in the image of God. We see their dignity, as people loved by God. This has large stakes. For example, a business owner who sees people in a generous way should ensure employees are fairly compensated and not overworked and underpaid, as Theary shared about her experience in the garment factory.

As my friend Pastor Josh Deeter says, a person's dignity isn't connected to what they own or produce, or the choices they make, or even what they are able to do. They have dignity because they are created in the image of God.

Developing a spirit of generosity helps us see people as God sees them. Nurturing generosity in our lives helps us have grace toward others, showing the love and mercy that we have received from God. Just as God's grace is given freely to us, we can share love and mercy with others "just because."

As Reverend Jim Lyon, General Director of Church of God Ministries and author of this book's foreword, told me, "Generosity begins with a balanced sense of self. This requires an understanding and receipt of grace. Grace brings a certain generosity of spirit that opens our hearts to engage, mend, and heal with others. It requires the art of forgiveness and the cognitive choice to believe the best, not the worst. Grace is an important concept in caring for others, including people living in poverty."

Generosity, then, includes relational generosity—how we relate to and with others. And, as we'll explore later in this chapter, this is related to our holiness. Generosity is a way of living. It's who we are. It's related to God's love for us and others.

Modeling Generosity

Not too long ago, when my wife and I were grocery shopping in our neighborhood in Istanbul, we each noticed a fifty-something man carrying a large plastic bag and a handful of coins. He was much shorter than me, and seemed to be noticing if people were noticing him. When we passed him the first time, he was counting his coins. He looked up at me quickly, embarrassed, as if he felt the world was looking down on him. I nodded my head and half-smiled, the way you do when you catch someone's eyes for a moment and you want to signal you acknowledge the person but you don't want to make things more awkward. I didn't want him to think I'd been staring.

I thought about how those coins were maybe all he had to buy his groceries. I wondered if he needed more money. Then I thought how people, especially in some cultures, like Turkey's, might be insulted if I offer money they don't feel they need. I reasoned with myself, *He may need money, but his personal honor could be insulted if I assume he's poor. I don't think he would want my money.* With those thoughts, I let myself off the hook. I listened to the beast of resistance, fed by an assumption the man wouldn't want anything from me. As we continued shopping, I didn't forget about him. *Will we see him in the next aisle? Will I feel compelled to help him?*

A few minutes later, my wife noticed him looking at tomato paste and vegetable oil—two important staples of Turkish cuisine. He studied the prices and looked down at his coins. Then he walked away. My wife pulled out her wallet and told me she was going to give him money.

I have asked her several times to help me be more generous. That day, she was modeling generosity, helping me be the person I want to be. Her generosity was also matched with discernment. In this case, she sensed this man's kindness—his goodness, she would tell me later—and she wasn't worried he'd take the money and run to the alcohol aisle. I felt relief—that she, as a Turkish person and woman, would help this man who I had convinced myself didn't need any help.

I'm not sure if it was the voice of reason or the beast of resistance, but I cringed at the amount she said she was going to give him. "I think that's too much," I said. We quickly agreed on an appropriate amount and she chased after him, money in hand.

"Here, I want to help you. Please take this," she told the man.

"Oh, I must have disturbed you when I was counting my money. I'm so sorry," he replied.

"No, you didn't disturb us." She held out the money. She could smell his body odor.

He took only half. "It's too much."

"We've all had difficulties, so please take it," my wife replied.

It was enough to convince him. "Thank you. Thank you. Thank you," the man said.

He walked back to the tomato paste and vegetable oil and selected the cheapest items on the shelf. Later, he was walking around with a multi-pack of small facial tissues, the kind poor people in Istanbul sell on the street. Women buy them to carry in their purse.

"He was so gentle, so humble," my wife said to me. "He didn't even want to accept all the money." She looked away and began to cry, overwhelmed by his need and demeanor. "It breaks my heart. He just has so little."

In contrast, we had a full cart, over a hundred dollars' worth of groceries and household items. Later, I felt that all we had purchased for ourselves belittled the few dollars we had given to the man. Yet, we had given to him something that enabled him to buy items he wouldn't have been able to buy on his own. And that felt good.

We left the store and began our short walk home. We saw the man again, standing alone, waiting for a customer to walk by to purchase one of the packs of facial tissues he'd just purchased. We greeted each other as we walked by, and he eagerly held out two packs of tissues. I didn't want to accept them, but my wife told me I needed to receive his token of appreciation. I told him we'd take one.

He smiled widely and thanked us again.

Encountering God through Generosity

I wonder, when we help those in need—financially or other-wise—if we're taken to a place within ourselves where we feel closer to God. In this way, we not only connect with those in need, but also allow God's love in us to grow and our love for others to expand.

As for my wife that day in the grocery store, I wonder if her act of kindness allowed her to encounter God in a new way, more deeply feeling God's heart for others and making her more holy. I think, by helping those in need, we're somehow changed—made more holy—through our acts of generosity. In short, being generous can lead us to a closer relationship with God.

Holiness is living a life that pleases God in the things we do and don't do. Holiness leads us to generosity, and generosity helps us to be holy. Yet, while there's a connection between helping others and feeling closer to God, it's more accurate to think in terms of obedience to God as making us holy, not simply acts of generosity. Holiness is living, and living out our faith, in a way that pleases God.

If my wife had stifled the feelings that led her to help the man in the grocery store—pushed them away like I had, with rationalization or excuses for not helping—she would not have been blessed by the encounter with God that resulted in helping someone. A few weeks later, she said she hoped we would see that man another time, so we could help him again.

Holiness Keeps Us Focused on the Needs of Others

Holiness is where the other Attitudes of the Helping Heart are rooted, allowing them to flourish. Holiness is keeping our hearts clean and in tune with God. If we aren't holy, we'll feel disconnected from God, which can disconnect us from others. This can impact the way we touch other people's lives.

Holiness is, of course, connected to our love for God. It is also linked to our sharing love with others. I've realized that sin not only steals peace and joy from me, but it can also steal something from other people. In my own heart, when sin replaces the Spirit of God, it feels as though the Spirit has left me and is no longer able to move through me and interact with others.

Without sin, I have a clear mind. I can think well. In contrast, sin stops me from positively impacting others. It stops me from sharing a friendly smile, from saying encouraging words, from thinking about the needs of others. It hinders my capacity, or God's capacity through me, to effect people. Sin takes away what I could freely give to others.

Since feeling closer to God can help us feel closer to others, holiness can lead us to greater generosity. It enables us to more easily love people. When we are holy, we are likely to be more compelled to be generous in different forms. We are more focused on God's love and concern for others. People and their needs stay in our hearts.

Returning to Shalom through Realigning Experiences

Another way of thinking of holiness is being in alignment with God. Alignment is shalom—complete peace and harmony—with God, others, and ourselves. However, in life, it's easy to get off track. Sometimes we focus more on the here and now, even if that's not what matters most. Because of this, we need to be intentional about seeking out what helps us be the person we want to be. We need to realign ourselves to where God wants us to be.

To do this, we need "realigning experiences." These are moments that call us to a closer relationship with

God—experiences that re-adjust us. They're like a spiritual tune-up. For me, this can occur when reading Scripture, when worshiping on Sunday, or when listening to a YouTube video.

One day, I sat at an outdoor café in my neighborhood in Istanbul, finishing my online Turkish lesson, as a large white street dog lay near my feet. I perused Facebook and saw the live feed of a church service from Main Street Church of God in Anderson, Indiana. Soon I was singing along quietly as the congregation sang a song I hadn't heard in years. The internet connection was spotty, and the live feed paused more than it played. Nevertheless, what I experienced—hearing the music, singing the words, recollecting good memories—was enough to help realign me with God, even if for a moment. Though brief, it was what I needed at that time. It was a realigning experience.

Realigning experiences are about engaging with something that helps us be the people we ultimately want to be. They help us in who we are becoming. They remind us of who we were, who we are, and who we ought to be. They remind us to keep God first. Realigning experiences serve as significant reminders of what is most important and how we need to live. They also help us remember our baptism.

One year, my wife and I attended Holy Week services in our old neighborhood in Oxford, England, at an Anglican church where chimes ring out each day from a tall bell tower. Inside, columns and arches frame each side of the nave, and a large gold icon of the sitting, crowned Christ is painted on the wall high above the altar. On Good Friday, a cross with the figure of Christ was placed in the center aisle. People lined up and kneeled down, one by one, kissing it before returning to their seats.

The next evening, we all stood outside the church, around a lit campfire—the fire representing Christ's victory over death and darkness. From this flame, a large Easter candle was lit, symbolizing the risen Christ. We followed this candle, procession style, into the church for the Easter vigil. Inside, we were invited to gather near the baptismal font for a re-affirmation of baptismal vows. The priest, in a white robe, dipped a leafy branch from a shrub into the water and flicked it in the air, as if he were cracking a leather horsewhip. I stood there, waiting to receive the sprinkles of water, waiting to be reminded of the sacredness of baptism. We felt the cool droplets on our faces and saw them on our clothes.

This was also a realigning experience, and I recalled the words of my theology professor, Dr. Gilbert Stafford, at Anderson University, who would talk about remembering one's baptism.

The world has always been a place where our thoughts and aspirations can easily drift away from God's good desire for us. It's easy to forget who we are and who we want to be. In such a state, we come to a place where we need to be realigned to God.

Realigning experiences can be critical to our faith and spiritual wellbeing. In the church that day, we were refreshed by baptismal waters, giving us an opportunity to recall the holy mystery of the spiritual washing of our sins. It prompted us to remember what we may have forgotten, helping us to be who God wants us to be.

Linking Prayer, Holiness, and Generosity

Holiness leads us to prayer, and prayer helps us to be holy. Prayer focuses us. It reframes our minds so we are fuller of God's love and less likely to step away from God. Prayer can help us feel gratitude, humility, empathy, and compassion. It can help us be more generous. Prayer ensures we tune our hearts to God and the things that matter to him.

Not too long ago, I was agitated with my wife over a couple of small things—the kind so minor that, when you look back, you feel ashamed about making a big deal out of nothing, if you can even remember what it was about. That evening before dinner, I prayed silently, "God, please help me be more generous to my wife. Help me to be gentle and kind to her, and understanding." In this case, I was praying for generosity in love. I then had a realization about generosity. I needed to pray to be generous, to ask God to help me be generous in big and small ways. On my own, I fail.

I believe being generous can make us happier. But I'll tell you a secret. I'm afraid to ask God to help me be generous about how to help others. I feel I'll have a big responsibility I won't want to accept. What will God ask me to do? What will be my response? It's a scary thing, talking to God about being generous.

Through prayer, we communicate with God. He speaks to us, quiets our minds. Through prayer, we ask for his help. We ask God to intervene, to do things for us we cannot do for ourselves. Yet, prayer also does something else. It changes us. Søren Kierkegaard and other theologians and pastors have emphasized how prayer can change the pray-er. In prayer, we tune into the heart of God, and this has the potential to change us. Shouldn't it? As pray-ers, shouldn't we be growing closer to God? Shouldn't *we* change as we ask God to answer our prayers?

Through prayer, we can change as we enter into an experience where our thoughts are aligned with God's desires. If we think of prayer as changing us, just as it can move God, then praying can also move us to develop a closer connection with people living in poverty, as God suffers along with those who experience difficulties. This helps us fight the beast of resistance within us that tells us not to be generous. It leads us to better help those in need.

Praying for generosity can change our hearts so we see opportunities to be generous as opportunities to share some of what we have been given. Of course, that doesn't mean we shouldn't be smart in what we give or to whom we give it. Discernment and wisdom are key aspects of giving wisely.

As we think and pray about those in need, we should remember that most people who are experiencing extreme poverty live in countries we'll never visit and villages we don't know exist. Prayer not only draws us to God; it can also help us feel closer to others, including those we'll never see. Praying can tie our hearts closer to the heart of God so we feel more sensitive to the needs of others, more aware of how to help them. Prayer helps develop within us an emotional and spiritual connection with people living in poverty, which can lead us to being generous. It helps us stay holy.

Generosity and holiness are deeply connected. While prayer helps us live a life of holiness, holiness inspires us to live a life of generosity, in all its many forms.

Taking It to the Next Level

Review the reflective questions, recite the prayer, read the Bible passage, take the challenge, and write your personal reflections in the free *7 Attitudes of the Helping Heart Companion Study Guide.*

Download the free study guide at:
http://www.johnchristopherframe.org

In the Words of Sak, the Security Guard

Reflections on life after monkhood

*A*fter my time as a monk, I went to another part of the country for a short time and worked at a restaurant, looking after cars and motorbikes. I then came to Phnom Penh to work in a garment factory for a couple of months. Because the salary was low and the conditions were hard, I stopped working there and began working for a security company. They didn't pay on time. It was one and a half to two months late, so it was hard working there. So, I started working for the security company I currently work for. It's been about three months now.

I got married while I was working at the first security job. Actually, though, we haven't gotten married yet. I mean we started living together, and we plan to get married. We tried to save money to get married. Then an emergency happened, and I needed to use the money for that, as well as for my family, and then we had a baby. We really want to get married, but we don't have money yet to do it.

In the Words of Theary,
the Garment Factory Worker

Reflections on life in a garment factory

I have a lot of friends in the factory. About four or five are close friends. They're in quality control too, so we work together.

I like my job, but sometimes it is boring, or there can be some challenges when checking the clothes, like the new models. I think the worst part of my job is when the new model comes. For the new model, I have to make sure everything is correct. I have to spend more than five minutes per shirt, inspecting each one. There are a lot of mistakes from the seamstresses, and if it has a problem, I have to send the clothes back. Then they fix it and send it back to me. I may even have to send it back again if it still has a problem. That is the worst part. Sometimes I feel bored and want to quit and find a new job.

My place is close to the factory, so I walk or go by motorbike. Some workers travel in the back of trucks about thirty miles from their village to get to the factory. These trucks carry fifty to seventy people, depending on how big they are. The workers who travel by truck—they're at risk because of accidents. There are a lot of accidents on the road on their way to work or going back home. Workers pay for this transportation, depending on how far they live from the factory.

Because the workers in the factory try to save money, they don't eat well. So, when they work, they can start having health problems because the food they eat is not healthy and they don't have enough energy to work as hard as they do. Some workers will only spend 12¢ to 25¢ for a meal. They'll spend 50¢ to 75¢ per day on food.

Chapter 7

Hope: Inspiring Belief and Action

In January 2004, *Dateline NBC* featured a televised report about child sex trafficking in Cambodia. The footage included young children propositioning an undercover reporter. In another part of town, a motorcycle taxi driver pulled up to the curb and told the reporter of a place with "many, many, many girls." Some were as young as twelve, he said.

Don and Bridget Brewster, who had just returned from Cambodia, watched the program. Don, a pastor in California, said it wasn't until that night that they learned about this problem. "I couldn't believe it was right under my nose and I didn't even know it," he said. "We have three daughters and six granddaughters, and we felt like if no one would help our daughters or granddaughters, how would we feel? We just felt like we needed to do something."

Don and Bridget talked with officials in Cambodia and experts on the ground about how they could help. They made a plan, sold their home, and moved to Cambodia, hoping to make a difference. Through their organization, Agape International Ministries, they developed a restoration home. It would help meet one of the greatest needs in Cambodia at that time: a safe place for trafficked and abused children.

Along with formal therapy, girls in their programs are told they have value, Don said. "When they begin to believe that Jesus loves them, that Jesus died for them, and that he has a plan for their life, you see the transformation from hopelessness to hopefulness. And it results in, 'I'm gonna go to school. I'm gonna do all I can do to be who God has called me to become.' That change from hopelessness to hopefulness is amazing to see."

Don and Bridget believed the best way to prevent trafficking was to tackle the problem holistically. That meant helping the wider community in different ways, including creating a safe space for children to gather. They soon developed a community center in the same neighborhood that had been featured in the *Dateline NBC* broadcast. The building had once been a brothel—a place of evil transformed into a place of hope. To this day, community members receive healthcare and education there, and a church service is held every Sunday morning.

Don and Bridget expanded further, opening a gym across the street to minister to traffickers. They also have a school for hundreds of children. They opened an employment center and factories that provide meaningful work. They organize small teams that go out to meet young women involved in sex work, inviting them to begin a new life with the support of their organization. Agape International Ministries now staffs four hundred Cambodians and dozens of long-term volunteers.

"Christ, through his church, will defeat the evil of sex trafficking," Don told me the first time we met. "We do everything we can to stop trafficking and share Christ's love to survivors. I really believe love is the way, including to the bad guys, not just the kids." He added, "That's not always easy. When these kids are rescued, they do not come well behaved. We try to express to them love by what we do and how we do it. We hope that, as Christians, Christ will be seen in us. It's not telling you that God loves you, but experiencing that love through you. There's no transformation in being told you're loved or being told you're special. It's experiencing it. Then you can begin to believe it."

"We actually have a girl who gave her testimony recently," Don continued. "She talked about being told she was special; she was told lots of times. But she said, 'I never believed that.' Then one day, because she was loved for four years, she said, 'I realized, I am special.'"

Don also told me the story of a grandmother who had visited the clinic in their community center because she had a headache. The staff gave her aspirin and she returned the next day to say thanks. "You guys helped me. What can I do to help you?" she asked. "I don't have any money. We're poor and I'm trying to take care of my granddaughter." The staff invited her to attend church services at the organization's facilities, and she did. They didn't know it yet, but the grand-mother's nine-year-old granddaughter was being raped. She couldn't keep her safe.

"Every Sunday," Don told me, "we talk about the value of children and the importance of stopping trafficking. We do that every Sunday in our church service, no matter what else we talk about." After five weeks, the grandmother returned to the clinic and said, "I'm going to trust your Jesus. You say Jesus wants to protect children. I'm going to tell you what's happening to my granddaughter."

A social worker took her statement, and the organization was given temporary custody of the granddaughter to keep her safe, allowing her to go through their program. "That would be pretty cool even if that was the end of the story," Don said. But it continues. "The girl's mom and dad and two siblings had been labor trafficked. They worked in a brick factory for a $700 loan from the factory owner. The father is an alcoholic and a gambler, and one day he decided to escape from the brick factory. He comes back to his home, leaving his wife and two kids there. He doesn't say anything to anybody, and just goes back to drinking."

Don went on, "The wife is told by the brick factory owner, 'Hey, I gave you a lot of money, and your husband is our best worker. I want him back. Here's twenty bucks. Get on the bus and bring your husband back here right now. To make sure you hurry, we're not gonna feed your kids while you're gone.' So, she comes back to their home and also says nothing. She's just back with her husband, leaving the two kids there, not being fed, working fourteen hours a day.

"The grandmother brings her to the church and explains what happened, and that the kids are still at the factory. Our social worker takes the statement and we go to the police, but they say it's not enough evidence. So, the social worker actually sneaks into the brick factory and takes photographs, records conversations, and gets somebody to feed the kids. We go back to the police with the new evidence, and they say, 'Okay, we'll go and get the kids.' The family is then reunited. That, too, would be pretty cool all by itself," Don said.

But the story continues again. Don concluded, "One of the girl's siblings who was working in the brick factory is her eight-year-old brother, and he's the cutest kid you ever saw. I mean, he's wearing farmer overalls, nothing else. His hair is spiked with clay, like Tom Sawyer. He gives the police enough information for them to do a raid of the entire brick factory. They rescue eighteen people, close it down, and the brick factory owner is still in prison today. Two aspirins did that! That's the whole point of everything we do."

Big Hope

Don and Bridget left their life in the United States to bring hope to a place once infamous for heinous crime. What drove them was not just a call to do something about a big problem. It was probably also a belief that they could make some difference. They had hope they could help. They had hope for the people they served.

Hope includes believing, with God, that our actions can make a difference. It's believing we can do something for others. That even if what we give or do is small, it can serve some good. Hope is an encouraging Attitude of the Helping Heart and is meaningful in many ways.

Hope is anticipation of something good. It is believing God can do something we can't do for ourselves. We hope God will do something great—heal the sick, help people in need, solve a problem. As Don Brewster said, they even hope Christ will eradicate trafficking. That's big hope.

Author and speaker Bob Goff, who introduced me to the problem of human trafficking through a talk at Anderson University, believes that hope and expectation are both rooted in anticipation. For Bob, hope means living constantly in anticipation and expectation. Though expectation sometimes gets a bad rap, he said, "Expect that God's going to do terrific things by you, through you, and hopefully because of you."[17] Therefore, hope is also believing God can use you.

Hope is also something we can share with others. When we inspire others with our own hope, they more easily can catch the vision we caught, or at least a piece of it, so they can do their part as well. In this way, having hope helps others to have hope. Our hope becomes an example for others, and they also have hope. The personal belief that I can make a difference is then transformed to a different vision: together we can make a difference, with God's help. Our hope is increased as we envision that together we can bring about some change.

My friend Pastor Josh Deeter says there is a tension

---

17 Mary Beth Thomas, "Thoughts on Hope," *Hello Hope*, September 15, 2015, https://hellohope.com/blog/thoughts-on-hope-bob-goff-interview.

between compassion and hope. "Compassion is rooted in now and what we can see. Hope is future oriented and what we anticipate seeing. Both drive you to action. Compassion drives you to action because things are not as they should be. Hope should drive you to action because you know what can or will be. You need both. You need to hold them in tension."

Pastor Josh says hope is about believing people can rise out of poverty if they're helped properly. "Hope sees potential in other people," he told me. "It's believing people don't have to be poor forever. Though there are extenuating circumstances, it's hoping changes will happen. Or hoping people will make changes that can help themselves. You don't want to just feed the poor. You want to help them so they won't stay poor. Hope is about what can be. What will be."

This kind of hope is about who people can become. It's about believing things can get better. To have this kind of hope, I think, not only requires faith in God's power and what God can do through you; it also requires an outlook on life that sees the future differently than others see it. It's looking at the world with hopeful eyes.

This kind of hope is what drives perseverance. If Don and Bridget Brewster would not have had hope, their perseverance may not have endured. Why persevere through difficulties, if there's no hope things will get better, even in a small way?

Hope Sustains Us

Hope is essential. It helps us get through life. It helps us help others. Those who are poor need and deserve hope. The rest of us need and deserve it as well, as it helps us stay focused on God. And it inspires us to help those in need. Hope isn't just something for me, or you, or people who are poor. Hope sustains all of us. Without hope, our impact, or the impact God can have through us, may be limited. And while hope is very much about today and tomorrow, it also helps us remember that this life is just a stepping stone into eternity. We often think of hope in terms of what theologians call "eschatological hope"—the hope of Christ's return and life in heaven.

Nicky Gumbel, vicar of HTB Church in London, said, "When I encountered Jesus, I found that, in him, there is hope. There's a hope, ultimately, of eternal life—that this life is not the end. Everything else is going to go—everything the world puts their hope in. But if your hope is in Jesus, that will never come to an end because that's a relationship that goes on forever. And we just have to remind ourselves in the dark times that this life is not the end, and that, ultimately, we have an eternal hope in Jesus. Jesus is the same, yesterday, today, and forever. He is our hope."[18] In this way, Jesus is the key to our hope for others here on earth.

As people of faith, we believe a new day will come when all the needs and problems of the world will go away. The hungry will be fed. The sick will be well. The poor will be rich. This eschatological hope, however, should not interfere with our hope that things can get better today. It shouldn't lead us to think, *Everything's going to be fine someday, so I don't need to worry about the needs of others today.* Instead,

---

18 Online interview with Nicky Gumbel, *HTB at Home*, September 27, 2020, https://www.htb.org/htb-at-home-catch-up.

eschatological hope can drive our worldly hope. It can inspire us to understand that what we have is not our own, that it is here today and gone tomorrow. It reminds us that our hope is not in things of the world, but in things we are yet to experience. This kind of hope strengthens our faith. It helps us live out our faith in a way that is mindful of others and their needs. It inspires us to be the people God wants us to be.

Hope and Action

Every year on April 23, thousands of Turks board ferries and make their way to a small island off the coast of Istanbul for an annual pilgrimage. Many of them purchase a spool of colorful thread from vendors to unravel as they walk up a steep cobblestone path to the top of a small mountain.

Interestingly, in a country where Islam is the religion of the vast majority, the people walk toward a Christian church, named after St. George, that overlooks the bright-blue Sea of Marmara and the coast of one of the world's largest cities. April 23 is remembered as St. George's Day around the world, but in Turkey, it is National Sovereignty and Children's Day. Those making the pilgrimage to the island are wishing, praying, and hoping for something specific, like a new job, money, or a baby.

When they finish their walk, they hang charms or ribbons in the trees of the churchyard. Some are tied on the shrubs along the walkway, perhaps placed by people who couldn't make the full journey up the mountain. A charm that looks like a tiny golden house is placed by somebody wanting a home. Charms of all sorts abound—for a car, good health, to find a spouse. People also light candles at the entrance of the church. One year, I saw a woman standing in front of the icons inside the church, touching each one with her wallet. I imagined she was praying for money, hoping her actions would make something happen that she couldn't make happen herself.

Among the thousands of people making wishes and saying prayers are others holding small boxes of white sugar cubes—the kind Turks drop into their tea and stir around with tiny spoons until they disappear. They hold the boxes out to people passing by, offering the sugar cubes as a symbol that their wish, made on that pilgrimage in a previous year, had come true.

In some ways, this was similar to when people in the church I grew up in would give testimonies—a few sentences about how God had worked in their lives. Testimonies were both a symbol of gratitude and also a way to bring hope to others in the congregation. One older man in our congregation, Charles, would often stand up and say, "I don't ever want to let an opportunity pass by to say something good about the Lord." Then he would share something about what had happened over the past week. If he didn't have anything specific to share, he would just say he was glad to be a Christian, or that even if he'd discover that heaven didn't exist, he'd still be a Christian because it was a better way of living.

On the island, by sharing sugar cubes, people celebrate something good that had happened in their lives. The sugar cubes are a symbol—a testimony—that the things they had wished for had become reality. Sharing them is a way of encouraging others, a way to extend hope to everyone else.

It would be easy to consider such a tradition folksy. For atheists, it's against reason. For the religious, it doesn't conform to anything from a holy book. Yet, people come every year, hoping, wishing, praying for something that they are unable to obtain on their own. They go to the island to do something, hoping something great might happen. They meet hope with action.

If they didn't do whatever it was they felt they needed to do—if they only hoped for their wish to come true—they probably wouldn't have much faith that it would. But they do something, even if they don't know why they're doing it. They go. They walk up the hill. They unravel the spool of thread. They light the candle. They buy the charm and hang it in a tree. They pray.

They do something in conjunction with their hope.

Just like the other Attitudes of the Helping Heart explored in this book—Empathy, Compassion, Gratitude, Humility, Generosity, and Holiness—Hope can grip our hearts in a way that we feel compelled to do *something*, even if we're not quite sure what that should be. While the other Attitudes of the Helping Heart are about today—how we're feeling now—hope is about what can be, as Pastor Josh said. What will be. Hope drives love and love drives hope.

"We have to hold onto hope because there's not much hope out there in the world right now," Nicky Gumbel said. "Christians are dealers in hope. And that's our calling—to bring people hope."

Hope goes beyond the other Attitudes of the Helping Heart. Like the others, it moves us, but in a different way. Hope empowers us to show God's love. Furthermore, it helps us see a better day for those in need. Hope reassures us we can make a difference. It assists us in alleviating hardships on earth while also looking to an eternity that doesn't have the problems we have today. Hope enables us to impact people spiritually. Hope inspires us, helping us to have faith that things can change. Hope encourages us to believe those who suffer can be comforted. That those who are poor can have their needs met, even if that's not until the next world. Hope motivates us to act, helping us live out our faith. It motivates our love.

Hope and action go hand in hand. Without hope, we may not feel like taking action. Without action, what we hope for may not happen. While hope is belief in what can be, it's rooted in action. Without it, hope isn't really hope.

Taking It to the Next Level

Review the reflective questions, recite the prayer, read the Bible passage, take the challenge, and write your personal reflections in the free *7 Attitudes of the Helping Heart Companion Study Guide*.

Download the free study guide at:
http://www.johnchristopherframe.org

In the Words of Sak, the Security Guard

Reflections on dreams

I would like a better life. I want to have my own house and my own things in the house, and I want a good income to support my family, so we can have a good life. I think a good income is around $250 to $300 per month. I think if I could earn that much salary, I could live a good life. I'd like a house similar to my family's house in the countryside, but I'd like it to be a bit bigger—the width would be about fifteen feet and the length about twenty-five feet. That's my dream. It would be made out of wood, and the windows wouldn't have glass.

There'd be a kitchen and toilet inside the house. I'd want to have a cabinet and a table and a TV on the table. I'd have a picture next to that. In the front of the house, there would be a room and a hall, and then a living room with the TV and everything there. Then there would be the bathroom and kitchen in the back. And there would be a wooden bed with a small, comfortable mattress. In the living room there would be another bed with a thin mat. This is my dream house to build in the future.

I'm not sure about the future yet. If I'm able, I will do it, but if not, it won't happen.

In the Words of Theary, the Garment Factory Worker

Reflections on hopes for the future

*M*y dream is to be a tailor—to design clothes. I'd like to quit working in the factory and have my own tailor shop where I design and make all kinds of clothes for women, men, and children. There's a school where I can learn how to become a tailor. I think it will take some time before I'm actually able to do it, but it's possible.

In the Words of Pun, the Great-Grandmother

Reflections on life

I '*m not really afraid of anything because I believe in Jesus. I would say that I've been happy throughout my life. My kids are taking good care of me. They visit me and give me food—and I can eat a lot.*

I have regrets, of course, but I leave all of that with God to decide. If I could do it all over again, I would have tried my best to help my kids more—provide them education and everything as much as possible.

I only have my kids and the church. Even though I'm not rich financially, I feel rich because I believe in God.

Chapter 8

Conclusion: Connecting Our Faith with the Needs of Others

In the fall of 1987, a forty-seven-year-old Sunday school teacher, JoAnn Bartholomew, was on her way home from a Wednesday evening church service when she was abducted and killed. The next day, her car was found in the parking lot of a shopping mall. Three days later, her body was found in a patch of woods.

Grief overwhelmed the people in her church. To honor JoAnn's love for others, they began a new ministry to help those in need. Now, decades later, JoAnn's Pantry, where all the food inside is free, continues to serve hundreds of families in Ohio each month.

Lawana Partlow and her husband, Jim, are the volunteer directors of JoAnn's Pantry. Before leading the pantry, Jim had served as a regular volunteer there for about ten years, and Lawana had helped out when she could. Lawana told me, "We just felt like we weren't able to be the directors. And God said you were, and that's the way it worked out. He just really spoke to our hearts and said, 'This is what you need to do.' God is in charge of the pantry."

Every Monday, Lawana and Jim pick up two to three tons of food from the local food bank and store it for the two give-out days they host at the end of each month. "It takes that long to get enough food," she said. The pantry—which is the size of a small grocery store—is staffed by volunteers, mostly people from the church but also some from the community. Families, scouts, high school students, and people from all walks of life serve those who come to pick up food, making them feel like they belong there.

"Some people tell you their story. Others don't," Lawana said.

Clients choose one of the two monthly give-out days to visit the pantry. When they arrive, volunteers chat with them and give out hugs. "If somebody comes in and has a need for prayer, we'll get a couple people to come together and we'll lay hands on them and pray right there," Lawana told me. "Some of the clients will join us in prayer for that person too." Lawana calls it joyful interaction. "People will ask each other, 'How have you been?' Somebody will say, 'I like your hair.' It's a place to feel connected, to get a little bit of support and community."

She continued, "If you need somebody to help you carry your groceries to the car, the guys are always willing to do that. They're like your neighbor or your friend who's helping you. It's not like it's a chore. It's a privilege. It's that attitude of service that makes the difference." The volunteers not only enjoy serving the people who come to the pantry; they also benefit from their relationships with other volunteers. "There's a very strong bond there. It's just a wonderful team of cooperative, helpful people."

"Before our give-out days begin, we start with prayer," Lawana said. "We pray for each other. We pray for the people who will come, that they will know we are Christians by our love. That we will be God's hands and feet while they are there." The volunteers serve everyone with kindness, like the elderly woman bent over with severe osteoporosis who is not much taller than her walker and has to turn her head to look up.

They also serve those who seem to hate the world. "You kind of want to love them the most because they are just kind of bristly. We only have a couple who we haven't broken through to," Lawana said. "There's such a sweet, sweet spirit there. The volunteers want to come back and they want to help. It is that spirit of relationship, because we don't serve the poor. We serve people. When you think of people as poor, it lowers them and it elevates you. And that puts up a barrier. And it can almost make you feel righteous."

However, at JoAnn's Pantry, nobody looks down on anybody. "We have this time together once a month with the people who come, and we share some resources with them. We check on them, and they check on us." When clients see Lawana and other volunteers in the community, they're not ashamed to come up to them and say, "Hey, I know you from JoAnn's Pantry."

"I think it's a very biblical service," Lawana told me. "The people who come to us have needs. It's not for us to judge why they're in the situation they're in. If you have a need, we should help. That's what we're trying to do. I know that if you want to have joy in your life, you have to be in the center of God's will. If you're doing what he wants you to do, you're going to have peace and fellowship with him and you're going to know that you're doing what you're called to do. We could be doing other things, but would we have the joy we have? Or would we be constantly chasing something else because of the hole that was left by being disobedient and not doing his will?"

Lawana's interest in volunteering with the food pantry may also stem from her own experiences of need. "I'm very empathetic because when I was a kid, we went and stood in line to get powdered eggs. My dad was disabled. He was paralyzed from the neck down, and my mom had two babies to take care of. I know what it's like to be on the other side of the table," she told me. "Sometimes you wish you could just tell people to trust God. Keep putting one foot in front of the other. Don't stop believing and moving forward. My parents kept trusting God and moving forward. I can definitely empathize with people who are going through a hard time. There's no shame."

Lawana explained the difference between people who are in financial poverty but are rich with relationships, and those who are poor both financially and without people to care about them. "The people who are truly poor are probably the most fragile community we have, and they need our service the most. They're the ones who come to the food pantry because they need a hug. They need someone who will tolerate their gruff exterior with compassion. Not only do they have a financial need or a need for food, they have a need for people and support and community. They are poor."

Lawana's hopes for the people they serve go beyond a desire to provide them food. She hopes what they do will open a door for people who visit the pantry to know Christ too, if they don't already. "We wish them health and prosperity," she said. "And if they can get to the point where they don't have a need, maybe they will become part of a community that will help to serve a need. I guess those are the things we could hope for anyone."

Begin by Doing Something

The volunteers of JoAnn's Pantry have been serving their community for thirty years. They put in countless hours. They connect with people in practical ways. They support them with their physical, emotional, and spiritual needs. They care, they serve, they help. They embody the Attitudes of the Helping Heart. They enjoy being together, sharing community with each other in service toward others. They're part of something bigger than themselves. Month after month, they are connecting their faith with the needs of others.

In this book, we've explored seven Attitudes of the Helping Heart—Gratitude, Humility, Empathy, Compassion, Generosity, Holiness, and Hope—that, when developed, can help you live out your faith so you can better care for those in need. Throughout this book, we've also heard the stories of individuals who have experienced poverty. This has allowed us to reflect on their hardships, as well as the similarities and differences between their lives and our own.

Caring for others is something many of us feel we need to do, and is modeled and taught throughout the Bible. For example, in the New Testament, the Parable of the Good Samaritan is a story of one man generously helping another, despite their being from people groups that despised each other. Another example is from the Old Testament, where the Israelites were instructed to leave some of their crops for those who were poor. Such a practical command reminded the Israelites that people in poverty should not be forgotten. That's an important lesson for us too.

In the introduction of this book, when considering the poverty and needs of others, we asked ourselves, "Where do we begin?" I think the answer is that we begin by doing *something*. And that begins with developing in our lives these seven Attitudes of the Helping Heart.

We know the solution to poverty is complex. We know that people who are hungry today will be hungry tomorrow. They need much more than daily food. Perhaps they're living in a country ravaged by war. Perhaps their crops haven't had sufficient rain. Perhaps they have family members dying from preventable diseases. Many of these problems are engrained in social structures that need revolution. They're steeped in bigger problems far deeper than what we see.

On a personal level, real problems in the world, like poverty, require us to grapple with challenging questions. To do that, we need the right mindset, nurturing in our lives Gratitude, Humility, Empathy, Compassion, Generosity, Holiness, and Hope. Developing these attitudes helps us to help others. They motivate us to learn more about the struggles of those living in poverty. They lead us to think about people who need our love and support.

As Christians, we often feel a burden to help those who are poor. We ponder how to do that, which might get in the way of actually doing something. Many times, we may not act at all. When that happens, maybe a little piece of us dies because we feel we're not living out our faith the way God wants us to.

Together, the seven Attitudes of the Helping Heart provide a framework that supports us on our journey of serving God and powerfully impacting others. When developed and lived out, they help us to fight the beast of resistance that keeps us self-centered—the opposition within ourselves that stops us from helping others.

The Attitudes of the Helping Heart work and flourish together. For example, embracing holiness helps us feel more compassion. Feeling gratitude helps us be more generous. Having empathy helps us experience greater humility. All of these attitudes are rooted in love—the love God has for all of us, and the love we can share with others. When developed in our lives, these attitudes empower us to better live out our faith and care for the poor.

Did you enjoy this book? You can make a big difference.

Reviews are important for authors to help them get the word out about their books. Accurate reviews of a book can help bring it to the attention of new readers. If you've enjoyed this book, it would be great if you could take five minutes and leave a review online. Thank you!

Bonus

Homeless at Harvard:
Finding Faith and Friendship on the Streets of Harvard Square

by John Christopher Frame

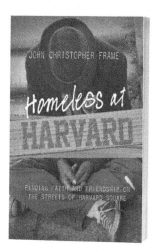

Introduction

I stood and gawked. Bundled in warm blankets and sleeping bags, people were asleep and nestled under the outdoor alcove of the Harvard Coop bookstore, across the street and about a hundred feet away from the gates of Harvard Yard. They were motionless, like bodies ready to be picked up by an undertaker; lonely, like campers expelled from an expedition.

I had decided to get off the subway to look around a place that was as foreign to me as the homeless individuals now sleeping in my presence. I was sightseeing that October night while in Boston for a conference. However, I wasn't expecting to see anything, or rather anyone, like this in Harvard Square, the business district around Harvard University.

Leaving Harvard Square that night, I didn't know if I'd ever walk by that bookstore again. Soon, though, I'd meet some of the people who had slept there. And less than two years later, I was sleeping there myself.

That night was similar to a night a year earlier in London, England, when I met a homeless man who was sitting on a sidewalk next to a King Rooster fast-food chicken restaurant. I had walked by him twice, and then wrestled with a voice within me telling me to turn around, go back, and offer him one of the two bananas I had just purchased at the corner market. I gave in to it.

As I approached the man, he reached out his hand and said in a British accent, "Sir, could you do me a favor? Here's five pounds. Will you go in there and buy me a dinner?" As he dropped the coins in my palm, I noticed that his hand was cold and chapped, cracked and seeping blood.

This was my first experience of meeting a homeless person, and he was giving me money, entrusting me with perhaps all the money he had. I asked him what he would like. "Chicken dinner" was all he said, in a broken, almost stuttering voice. When I returned with his meal, we talked for a while on the sidewalk, his two-liter bottle of white cider beside him. We shared the same first name, and I learned that John had a debilitating muscular disease, a teenage son, and a mother he loved but had not seen in a long time.

John sat on the sidewalk and his cane rested against the restaurant. Passersby gave him coins, which he graciously accepted, and after a few minutes, a man and a woman joined us. John openly shared with us about his troubles. He cried as we prayed together, as if his brokenness — or maybe it was hopelessness — needed to be heard. Though I left John that night to return to the comforts of my privileges, our brief encounter stayed with me.

∾

I grew up in a red brick house with a large, narrow lawn that my friends and I imagined as a major league baseball field. All summer long we played baseball with a yellow plastic bat and ball, trying to hit the ball over the fence into the church parking lot behind the parsonage where I lived. I announced every hit and strikeout as if I were broadcasting it like the radio voice of the Detroit Tigers, Ernie Harwell, and we dreamed of being as good as the players pictured on our bubblegum cards. Then we'd ride our bikes and play cops and robbers with my collection of cap guns and metal handcuffs, which looked as genuine as the ones in the police shows on TV. Because my dad was the pastor of a small church and my mom was a part-time teacher, my sister and I didn't grow up in a rich family. We had everything we needed, though, and most things any boy would hope to have, like a Nintendo, a cocker spaniel named Dixie who was my best friend, a newspaper route, and a fishing pole and a tackle box. Each night, I'd help set the table that my family gathered around for a homemade meal, and I was in our church several times each week. Besides seeing a few people around our city who looked down and out, I really knew nothing about homelessness.

In my late twenties, while pursuing a master's degree at Anderson University School of Theology, I felt inspired to get to know those who were living on the streets. My friends at Anderson, the author of a book I had read, and spring break trips to Atlanta to serve with a homeless ministry there helped me better understand how Christians should be concerned about the poor.

The day after I moved into my dorm on Harvard's campus in 2008 to begin a theology degree, I met a homeless man, George, sitting near his bedding, which was strewn out in front of a bank in Harvard Square. George helped me learn more about homelessness, as did some of his friends, such as Chubby John. I began spending time with them and also volunteering at the student-run Harvard Square Homeless Shelter, partly to fulfill a requirement for a Poverty Law class I was enrolled in. I began learning more about homelessness and about the relationships that help homeless people survive on the streets.

In a leadership class I took at Harvard, my professor taught us about translating life experiences into new actions that serve a greater purpose. I thought some more about how what I was learning about homelessness could be translated into something that could benefit others. For a long time, I'd wanted to write a book that could somehow make a difference, and I thought that by sharing my experiences with homeless people more broadly, I could help others think about building relationships with people on the streets.

It seems that those who do not know homeless people are often unaware of their circumstances and struggles. In general, many of us are unaware of how the homeless view themselves and their difficulties. We're unaware of how similar we are to individuals who are panhandling on the sidewalk. A glimpse of the experiences of those who live on the streets could help change that, I thought.

The thought of temporarily staying on the streets with the homeless had begun to grow in my mind since my second spring-break trip to Atlanta. So while taking my final class at Harvard during the summer of 2009, I took the plunge and slept outside among the homeless community for ten weeks. I didn't do it as a way to emulate Christ or to show that living on the streets is more righteous than living in a home. And I didn't do it in an effort to save people on the streets from their homelessness. Rather, I hoped it would give me a chance to learn about homelessness as an insider, which would better enable me to write about the stories and struggles of those who were really homeless; and I could share what it was like to spend a summer on the streets.

This book is not a story about me as a homeless person, for I was never truly homeless. Rather, it's a story about a homeless community and how my life and the lives of those on the streets were woven together into a special tapestry.

For me, hanging out on the streets was only temporary. I did not give up one life to embrace another. I could not put aside the fact that I had a loving family, and that I was a student at Harvard Divinity School with access to Harvard buildings, books, and bathrooms that my homeless friends didn't have access to. But despite having privileges that my homeless friends didn't have, they accepted me, just like they accepted each other. The gap between us didn't seem to matter. The homeless community befriended me and shared with me some of the wisdom they'd gained from years of living in their culture.

The ten weeks I spent on the streets provided me with an experience I'd never had before. It gave me a chance to begin new friendships and to deepen relationships with people I already knew, such as Dane. Dane was a former cocaine addict and notorious criminal who'd had an epiphany after losing one of his toes, setting him in a new direction. However, he remained on the streets. Another was Neal, who had been sleeping outside for many years in Harvard Square. Over the summer, he and I talked about life and love, friendship and faith. Although he claimed to live a happy-go-lucky life, by the end of the summer, I learned about the health problems that he endured.

In this book, you're going to meet some of those friends, such as Neal, Dane, Chubby John, and George.

Welcome to the community of the homeless at Harvard.

You may continue reading *Homeless at Harvard* in audio, ebook, or paperback, available at your favorite book retailer, or by visiting http://www.homelessatharvard.com.

Praise for

Homeless at Harvard:
Finding Faith and Friendship on the Streets of Harvard Square

"John challenges us to change...with his help, we learn something of the compassion Jesus asked of us..."

– Dr. Tony Campolo

"The book is touching, and well worth the read..."

– Publishers Weekly

"...a great read...hard to put down."

– Dr. John Aukerman

Made in the USA
Las Vegas, NV
26 February 2021